THE ICING ON THE CAKE

THE
ICING
ON THE
CAKE

YOUR ULTIMATE STEP-BY-STEP GUIDE TO DECORATING BAKED TREATS

Juliet Stallwood

DUNCAN BAIRD PUBLISHERS

LONDON

THE ICING ON THE CAKE
Juliet Stallwood

First published in the United Kingdom and Ireland in 2013 by
Duncan Baird Publishers, an imprint of
Watkins Publishing Limited
Sixth Floor
75 Wells Street
London W1T 3QH

A member of Osprey Group

Managing Editor: Grace Cheetham
Editors: Alison Bolus and Krissy Mallett
Art Direction and Design: Manisha Patel
Production: Uzma Taj
Commissioned Photography: Jon Whitaker
Food Stylist: Juliet Stallwood
Prop Stylist: Lucy Harvey

A CIP record for this book is available from the British Library

ISBN: 978-1-84899-065-4

10 9 8 7 6 5 4 3 2 1

Typeset in Century Old Style and Segoe Condensed
Colour reproduction by XY Digital
Printed in China

Publisher's note
While every care has been taken in compiling the recipes for this book,
Watkins Publishing Limited, or any other persons who have been involved
in working on this publication, cannot accept responsibility for any errors
or omissions, inadvertent or not, that may be found in the recipes or text,
nor for any problems that may arise as a result of preparing one of these
recipes. If you are pregnant or breastfeeding or have any special dietary
requirements or medical conditions, it is advisable to consult a medical
professional before following any of the recipes contained in this book.

Notes on the recipes
Unless otherwise stated:
Use fresh ingredients
Do not mix metric and imperial measurements
1 tsp = 5ml 1 tbsp = 15ml 1 cup = 250ml

DEDICATION
For my boys

Contents

Introduction

I am sitting writing this introduction at an old pine table in the café of our village shop in Dorset. My bakery is on the first floor, with its shiny worktops, ovens and racks. The window of the bakery looks out over our village primary school, church and my house, with the hills of the Cranbourne Chase in the distance. It's a very inspirational place in which to live, bake and decorate.

My family moved to Dorset from West Sussex, where I had been working as a graphic designer with my brother and his wife. It was here that our boys, now 15 and 13, were born. As they grew up I always looked forward to making their birthday cakes, and it was these early creations that sparked my love of cake decorating. I started out making novelty cakes, which I would base on the latest craze the children were into. Soon I started to get requests from friends and family for different, sometimes more challenging, cakes. I always felt that the last cake I had made was a bit better than the one before. I learnt something new with each project, and even though I had only read about cake decorating, it seemed to come quite naturally to me.

Over the next few years, cake decorating continued to be a hobby that I thoroughly enjoyed. I loved the whole process – the designing, the baking and, of course, the decorating. However, I always received the most pleasure, and still do, from seeing the recipient's face or receiving a thank you email telling me how delighted they were. On moving to my village, I fitted cake making for family and friends around other commitments. I was working less as a freelance graphic designer and started to bake more and more. My involvement with the primary school meant I could hold more cake sales – always a winner on the playground. I used these sales to apply techniques that I had learnt from my party-pleasing novelty cakes to smaller cupcakes. I am always excited by the opportunity to try out new ideas. Even now, as soon as a friend mentions they are holding an event, from a wedding to a tea party, I jump in there and ask if I can be of any help, or to put it plainly, "Can I make you a cake?"

As my cakes became more sophisticated, I started to pay more and more attention to detail. In autumn 2010, I saw a picture of some biscuits that had been iced in a highly decorative style. I had never seen anything like them before, and knew I had to try the technique for myself. An opportunity presented itself when I went to a meeting at my sons' school to discuss its forthcoming Christmas Market. Without even thinking, I volunteered to take a stall selling iced biscuits.

Having taken the plunge, I started thinking about what I was actually going to make. I also began dreaming about the image I wanted to project to the customers I hoped would come flocking to my stall. I didn't want them to think that I had just made a few biscuits to sell at the fair, and that was that. I wanted them to understand that baking and decorating was something I was passionate about. Endless biscuit making was coupled with designing decoration schemes on the computer. I experimented day after day and by the time the market came along, I had everything organized. One customer simply could not believe that just a few weeks previously I had never even baked a biscuit before. This was the turning point when I decided that I wanted to turn my baking and decorating into a business.

The following months flew by as I spent hours sitting at the kitchen table drawing up ideas for Valentine's Day and Easter ranges. It was very early on in my new career, but I took the step of setting up a website (with a little help from my family), which increased my potential clientele. Cakes were tricky as they could only realistically be sold to local customers. Still, cake baking and decorating continued in earnest, and also went hand in hand with other little treats, like macarons and fondant fancies. Biscuits, on the other hand, opened the door to the world – they can be posted anywhere – and over the next year I started to develop and refine my own techniques with every new design.

In the beginning, the books I read inspired me to practise and improve, and eventually to have the confidence to create my own designs and techniques. Baking and decorating presents endless possibilities. Nearly any image you can think of can be made into a cake or a biscuit, from a ghost to a teapot and from a hen to a handbag. The designing is always exciting – a few quick sketches, a little colour, a few embellishments, and there it is. The decorating process can often involve many stages, and patience is needed along with a steady hand. But once you see how each new project comes to life as the last drop of icing is added, I know you'll agree it's well worth the wait.

I love what I do and I love sharing my passion. I began running courses at the bakery so I could teach other enthusiasts the essential skills and techniques I have picked up along the way. This book is an extension of that goal – helping you to learn at your own pace, in your own time and in your own home.

Designs don't have to be complicated to look effective, in fact the simplest ones are often the best. There are projects in this book for the decorating novice that are very quick and easy to do, and others that may take a bit more time to master. In Chapter One, "Decorate to Indulge", you'll find lots of ideas for simple sweet treats for any day of the week. Chapter Two, "Decorate for Love", revels in the art of romance and includes inspiring ideas for occasions like weddings, anniversaries and Valentine's Day. Chapter Three, "Decorate to Celebrate", is full of treats to make birthday parties, baby showers and holiday festivities extra special. Chapter 4 is my *pièce de résistance*, "Decorate to Impress", where you'll discover how to make extravagant centrepieces that will amaze your family and friends.

Whatever your level of expertise, this book will help you bring out plate after plate of beautifully decorated goodies. It's the icing on the cake.

Juliet Stallwood

CHAPTER ONE

You don't have to wait for a special occasion to decorate sweet treats. With a little time and a few basic tools, you can easily turn a small family gathering on a Sunday afternoon or tea with friends into something more indulgent. It could be as simple as Chocolate-Dipped Florentines, as delicious as Decadent Fruit Tarts or as stunning as the Rose Swirl Cupcakes. Go on! Have your cake and eat it.

DECORATE
TO
INDULGE

Sugared Rose Petal Cake

MAKES 1 CAKE
petals from 1–2 edible pink or
red roses
1 large egg white, lightly beaten
125g/4½oz/heaped ½ cup
caster sugar
2 x 15cm/6in round Vanilla
Sponge Cakes (see pages
62–3)
½ recipe quantity Vanilla
Buttercream (see page 16)

YOU WILL NEED
small paintbrush
tray lined with baking
parchment
15cm/6in round cake drum

TIP
The crystallized rose petals can
be stored in an airtight container
lined with baking parchment for
up to 1 week. Do not store in the
fridge or they will become soggy.

1 Carefully separate the petals from the rose(s), taking care not to bruise them as you do so. Using the paintbrush, gently brush the petals to remove any debris. Discard any petals that are damaged or discoloured. Transfer the petals to the prepared tray.

2 Lightly brush the egg white over both sides of each petal with the paintbrush **(a)**, making sure they are completely coated – if sections of the petals remain uncoated, the sugar will not stick and you will be left with an uneven finish.

3 Pour the sugar into a bowl. Holding one of the petals over the bowl, gently sprinkle a little sugar over the petal with a teaspoon **(b)**, making sure it is completely coated. Shake off any excess sugar and place the petal back on the prepared tray. Repeat until all the petals are coated. Leave the petals to dry overnight, uncovered, at room temperature.

4 Following the instructions on page 150 and using the cake drum as a firm base, layer the cakes, then fill with buttercream to make one tall cake. Following the instructions on page 152, cover the cake with the remaining buttercream. Chill in the fridge for 2 hours.

5 When the buttercream has set and the petals have dried and become hard, carefully transfer the covered cake to a cake stand or serving plate and scatter the petals over the top.

(a)

(b)

Chocolate Swirl Mini Cupcakes

MAKES 24 CUPCAKES
50g/1¾oz plain chocolate
    candy coating
½ recipe quantity lilac-coloured
    Vanilla Frosting (see page 118)
24 Chocolate Sponge Mini
    Cupcakes baked in foil mini
    cupcake cases (see page 129)
½ recipe quantity turquoise-
    coloured Vanilla Frosting
    (see page 118)

YOU WILL NEED
chocolate swirl designs
    (see page 162)
A4 sheet of paper
baking parchment
piping bag fitted with a no. 2
    plain nozzle
piping bag fitted with a
    10mm/½in open-star nozzle

TIP
Candy coating is widely available online. You can buy it in various colours and in a variety of flavours including dark, milk and white chocolate. Candy coating is easy to use because, unlike chocolate, it does not need to be tempered. Heating and cooling chocolate without controlling the temperature (tempering) causes blemishes to appear on the surface. The chocolate will also crumble rather than snap.

1 Trace 24 chocolate swirl designs onto the sheet of paper and lay a sheet of baking parchment over the top **(a)**.

2 Put the candy coating in a heatproof bowl and rest it over a saucepan of gently simmering water, making sure the bottom of the bowl does not touch the water. Heat, stirring occasionally, until melted. Alternatively, put the coating in a microwavable bowl and microwave, uncovered, on medium for 2 minutes until melted, stirring every 30 seconds to ensure the coating does not overheat. The candy coating should have a smooth pouring consistency similar to double cream.

3 Spoon the melted candy coating into the piping bag fitted with the no. 2 plain nozzle. Carefully pipe over the outline of each swirl **(b)** to make 24 chocolate swirls. (For tips on piping, see pages 157–9.) Leave the chocolate swirls to one side for at least 10 minutes until the coating has completely set – you can transfer the chocolate swirls to the fridge to speed this process up, if you like.

4 Spoon the lilac frosting into the piping bag fitted with a 10mm/½in open-star nozzle and pipe a high swirl onto half of the mini cupcakes (see page 157). Clean the piping bag and repeat with the turquoise frosting until all of the mini cupcakes have been frosted with a swirl.

5 Gently lift one of the chocolate swirls from the baking parchment with a knife, handling it carefully as it will be very delicate. Place it on top of one of the frosted cupcakes, gently pressing it into the frosting with your finger. Repeat until all the mini cupcakes are topped with a chocolate swirl.

(a)

(b)

Basic Buttercream

MAKES 500G/1LB 2OZ
250g/9oz/2 cups icing sugar
250g/9oz salted butter, softened
food colouring pastes (optional)

YOU WILL NEED
electric mixer
cocktail stick (optional)

TIP
1 recipe quantity makes enough
buttercream to cover a 20cm/8in
cake, 12 cupcakes or 24 mini
cupcakes. (For quantities for filling
and covering different cake sizes
with buttercream, see page 155.)

Buttercreams help to keep cakes moist and are often used to fill and cover cakes before icing with sugar paste. They can be made in a variety of flavours to complement different sponge recipes (see below). Plain, vanilla and citrus buttercreams can also be coloured with food colouring pastes. To colour, simply add a small amount of food colouring paste to the mixture using the end of a cocktail stick, and mix until combined. Repeat until the desired colour is achieved. (For tips on filling and covering cakes with buttercream, see pages 150 and 152.)

For basic buttercream, sift the icing sugar into a mixing bowl. Add the butter and beat with the electric mixer for 5 minutes until pale, light and fluffy.

Variations

Cappuccino Buttercream: beat in 2 tsp (or more to taste) of coffee extract with the icing sugar and butter.
Chocolate Buttercream: use 220g/7¾oz/heaped 1¾ cups icing sugar and 30g/1oz/¼ cup cocoa powder, then beat together with the butter.
Citrus Buttercream: beat in the finely grated zest of 1 large lemon or 1 orange with the icing sugar and butter.
Mocha Buttercream: use 220g/7¾oz/heaped 1¾ cups of icing sugar, 30g/1oz/¼ cup cocoa powder and add 1 tsp (or more to taste) of coffee extract.
Vanilla Buttercream: beat in 2 tsp of vanilla extract with the icing sugar and butter.

Chocolate Ganache

MAKES 600G/1LB 5OZ
300g/10½oz semi-dark
   chocolate, at least 53% cocoa
   solids, broken into pieces,
   or chocolate drops
300ml/10½fl oz/1¼ cups double
   cream

TIPS
If the mixture splits, warm up a
little more cream, add it to the
mixture and stir until smooth.

1 recipe quantity makes enough
chocolate ganache to cover a
20cm/8in cake or 12 cupcakes.
(For quantities for covering
different cake sizes with chocolate
ganache, see page 155.)

1 Put the chocolate in a heatproof bowl. Rest the bowl over a saucepan of gently simmering water, making sure the bottom of the bowl does not touch the water. Heat, stirring occasionally, until melted. Alternatively, put the chocolate in a microwavable bowl and microwave, uncovered, on medium for 2 minutes until melted, stirring every 30 seconds to ensure the chocolate does not burn.

2 Pour the cream into a saucepan and bring to the boil slowly over a low heat. Pour the hot cream over the melted chocolate. Whisk until smooth and thickened, but take care not to overmix or the mixture will split.

3 Allow the ganache to cool for 10 minutes or until it is just starting to set, before using. Any leftover ganache can be stored in an airtight container in the fridge for up to 1 month.

Decorate to Indulge 17

Use this buttercream recipe for the following recipes throughout this book:

**Sugared Rose
Petal Cake**
page 12

**Fresh Flower
Fondant Fancies**
page 18

Chocolate Fan Cake
page 30

Valentine Cigarillo Cake
page 48

**Chocolate Box Cake
with Truffles**
page 52

**Pom Pom
Wedding Cake**
page 60

Dragon Cake
page 74

**White Blossom
Christening Cake**
page 84

Mini Ghost Cakes
page 91

Festive Ball Cakes
page 92

**Christmas
Pudding Cake**
page 97

Butterfly Fancies
page 116

Teapot Cake
page 122

Rose Cupcakes
page 126

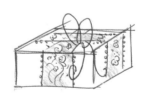

Gift-Wrapped Cake
page 135

Daisy Chain Mouse Cake
page 136

Use this chocolate ganache recipe for the following recipes throughout this book:

Chocolate Fan Cake
page 30

Ivory Corsage Wedding Cake
page 114

Fresh Flower Fondant Fancies

MAKES 16 FANCIES
18cm/7in square Vanilla Sponge
    Cake (see pages 62–3), cooled
1 recipe quantity Vanilla Sugar
    Syrup (see page 119)
½ recipe quantity Vanilla
    Buttercream (see page 16)
2 heaped tbsp seedless
    raspberry jam
icing sugar, for dusting
175g/6oz marzipan
2 tbsp apricot jam
600g/1lb 5oz/heaped 4¾ cups
    fondant icing sugar
ivory food colouring paste
lilac food colouring paste
16–20 fresh edible flowers,
    such as campanulas or violets

YOU WILL NEED
cake leveller or long serrated
    knife
pastry brush
palette knife
rolling pin
5mm/¼in marzipan spacers
    (optional)
sharp knife
icing smoother
ruler
long serrated knife
tray lined with baking
    parchment
16 foil or paper cupcake cases
piping bag

TIPS
If the marzipan sticks to the
rolling pin, dust the pin with a
little icing sugar before continuing
to roll.

For the best results, cook the
vanilla sponge cake the day
before it is needed, then wrap it
in baking parchment and foil and
leave it to rest overnight to firm
up a little – this will make it easier
to cut.

1 Chill the cake in the fridge for at least 1 hour until very cold and firm – this will make the sponge easier to cut. Using the cake leveller, level the top of the cake, then slice it in half horizontally. Brush the cut-side of each layer with sugar syrup, then spread a thin layer of buttercream over the top of one layer and a thin layer of raspberry jam over the other with the palette knife. Carefully sandwich the two layers together, then wrap the cake in cling film and chill in the fridge for at least 30 minutes, ideally 2 hours. (For tips on layering and filling cakes, see page 150.)

2 Meanwhile, dust the work surface with a little icing sugar, then knead the marzipan until smooth. Roll out the kneaded marzipan until it is 5mm/¼in thick, using marzipan spacers if you like, and cut out a square large enough to cover the top of the cake.

3 When the cake has chilled, remove from the fridge and unwrap the cling film. Warm the apricot jam in a small saucepan over a low heat, stirring occasionally, until it has a smooth, spreadable consistency. Alternatively, put the apricot jam in a small microwavable bowl and microwave, uncovered, on medium for 20 seconds. Brush the top of the cake with a thin layer of the jam, then gently place the rolled marzipan on top of the cake, taking care not to stretch or pull it. Smooth the marzipan with your hands, then smooth again with the icing smoother to achieve a flat level surface.

4 Trim the sides of the cake and cut out a large square measuring 16 x 16cm/6¼ x 6¼in. Using the sharp knife, score the marzipan into 16 equal squares about 4cm/1½in each, then use the serrated knife to cut down through the marzipan and cake to make 16 small square cakes. Transfer the cakes to the prepared tray, then cover with cling film and leave to chill in the fridge until needed.

5 Mix up half of the fondant icing according to the packet instructions in a deep heatproof bowl. Add a small amount of ivory food colouring paste and stir until thoroughly combined. Repeat until the desired colour is achieved. Rest the bowl over a saucepan of gently simmering water until it has a smooth pouring consistency similar to double cream. Alternatively, put the fondant icing in a microwavable bowl and microwave, uncovered, on medium for 1 minute.

6 Remove half of the cakes from the fridge. Following the instructions on page 151, cover a cake in ivory fondant icing and wrap in a cupcake case, then leave to one side until the icing has completely set. Repeat to make eight ivory fondant fancies in total. Repeat steps 5 and 6 with the remaining fondant icing, lilac food colouring paste and the remaining cakes to make 16 fondant fancies in total. Store any remaining fondant icing in an airtight container and leave to one side until needed – the icing will start to set as it cools.

7 When the fancies have set, spoon some of the remaining fondant icing into the piping bag, then snip off the tip if necessary. Pipe a small dot of icing on top of each fancy, then place an edible flower on top.

Sprinkle Whoopie Pies

MAKES 12 PIES
200g/7oz/scant 1 cup caster
  sugar
240g/8½oz salted butter,
  softened
1 large egg, beaten
280ml/10fl oz/scant 1¼ cups
  buttermilk
2 tsp vanilla extract
185g/6½oz/1½ cups plain flour
1 tsp bicarbonate of soda
70g/2½oz/heaped ½ cup cocoa
  powder
225g/8oz/1¾ cups icing sugar
210g/7½oz marshmallow fluff
60g/2¼oz white nonpareils or
  hundreds and thousands

YOU WILL NEED
electric mixer
4.5cm/1¾in spring-action-
  release ice cream scoop
  (optional)
2 baking sheets lined with
  baking parchment, plus extra
  baking parchment for relining
  the baking sheets
palette knife
piping bag

1 Preheat the oven to 170°C/325°F/Gas 3. Put the sugar and 115g/4oz of the butter in a mixing bowl and beat with the electric mixer until light and fluffy. Gradually beat in the egg, followed by the buttermilk and 1 teaspoon of the vanilla extract – if the mixture starts to curdle, add a little bit of the flour. Sift the flour, bicarbonate of soda and cocoa powder into the bowl, then beat gently until just combined. Cover the bowl with cling film and chill in the fridge for 30 minutes until firm.

2 Working in batches, scoop out 12 golf-ball-sized balls of the mixture with the ice cream scoop or tablespoon and drop them onto the prepared baking sheets, spacing them about 6cm/2¼in apart to allow each one to spread slightly during cooking. Cover the remaining mixture with cling film and return it to the fridge while you cook the first batch. Bake the prepared pies for about 10 minutes or until the tops spring back slightly when gently pressed with a finger. Remove from the oven.

3 Without removing the sponge halves, slide the sheets of baking parchment onto wire racks and leave to cool completely. Meanwhile, reline the baking sheets with baking parchment and repeat steps 2 and 3 with the remaining mixture.

4 To make the filling, sift the icing sugar into a clean mixing bowl, then add the remaining vanilla extract and butter and beat with the electric mixer for 2 minutes until smooth. Add the marshmallow fluff, then beat for about 3 minutes until light and fluffy.

5 Gently remove the sponge halves from the baking parchment with the palette knife. Spoon the filling into the piping bag, then snip off 1cm/½in from the tip if necessary. Pipe a flat swirl of filling onto the flat-side of one sponge half – starting from the edge and swirling the filling towards the centre. Sandwich together the piped sponge half with a plain sponge half to make a whoopie pie.

6 Pour the nonpareils into a small, shallow bowl. Holding the whoopie pie over the bowl, gently sprinkle the nonpareils over the edge of the filling with a teaspoon, turning the pie as you do so to ensure the filling is completely covered – if sections of the filling remain uncovered you will be left with an uneven finish. Shake off any excess nonpareils and transfer the whoopie pie to a plate. Filling and decorating one pie at a time, repeat steps 5 and 6 with the remaining sponge halves, filling and nonpareils until the edges of all the whoopie pies are covered in nonpareils.

Rose Swirl Cupcakes

MAKES 12 CUPCAKES
**12 Chocolate Sponge Cupcakes,
baked in foil cupcake cases
(see page 129)**
**1 recipe quantity pale pink-
coloured Basic Frosting (see
page 118)**

YOU WILL NEED
small serrated knife
**piping bag fitted with a large
closed-star nozzle**
**12 paper lolly sticks about
15cm/6in long**
vase and fresh foliage (optional)
lengths of ribbon (optional)

TIPS
To achieve a rose-like effect, you
need to keep the swirl as flat as
possible, so try not to overlap the
icing as you pipe.

Do not pour water in the vase if
using real foliage as the paper
lolly sticks will become soggy and
unable to support the cupcakes.

1 Using the serrated knife, trim off the domed top of each cupcake to create a level surface.

2 Spoon the frosting into the piping bag. Pipe a flat swirl (see page 157) over each cupcake –
starting from the centre of the cupcake **(a)** and swirling the frosting around the edge **(b)**. (For
tips on piping, see pages 157–9.)

3 Pierce a hole in the centre of each cupcake base with a skewer, pushing it through the foil case
and about 2.5cm/1in into the cake. Insert one of the lolly sticks into the holes, then place the cakes
in a vase with some fresh foliage to create a bouquet centrepiece, if you like. Alternatively, decorate
each cupcake stick with lengths of ribbon.

(a)

(b)

Gingerbread Family

MAKES 12 BISCUITS
icing sugar, for dusting
50g/1¾oz brightly coloured sugar paste in one or more colours (see pages 160–1)
100g/3½oz white soft-peak Royal Icing (see page 46)
12 biscuits made using 1 recipe quantity Gingerbread Biscuit Dough (see page 27), cut out with the gingerbread family templates (see page 163)
edible glue (optional)
edible glitter (optional)

YOU WILL NEED
small rolling pin
15mm/⅝in and 10mm/½in circle cutters
cocktail stick
palette knife
tray lined with baking parchment
piping bag fitted with a no. 2 plain nozzle
small paintbrush (optional)

TIPS
If you do not have a 10mm/½in circle cutter, use the flat top of a pencil, covered in a tiny piece of cling film, to indent the buttons.

You will need to make the buttons at least a day before they are needed. Try making flower- or heart-shaped buttons instead.

1 Dust the work surface with a little icing sugar, then knead the sugar paste(s) until soft and pliable. Roll out the kneaded sugar paste(s) quite thinly. To make the buttons, stamp out 2 circles per large biscuit and 1 circle per small biscuit with the 15mm/⅝in circle cutter.

2 While the sugar paste buttons are still soft, position the 10mm/½in circle cutter over the centre of each one and gently press it down to indent a circle into the buttons **(a)**. Do not cut through the sugar paste completely. Using the cocktail stick, prick 4 holes into the centre of each indented circle to create a button effect **(b)**. Using the palette knife, carefully transfer the sugar paste buttons to the prepared tray. Leave them to dry overnight, uncovered, in a cool, dry place.

3 When the buttons have dried, spoon the royal icing into the piping bag. Pipe a gingerbread person outline onto the top of each gingerbread person, then pipe a face onto each one. You can also pipe items of clothing onto the biscuits, if you like (see picture). To attach the buttons, pipe small dots of icing onto the centre of the biscuits, then place a sugar paste button on top. Leave the biscuits for at least 30 minutes in a cool, dry place, to allow the icing to set.

It's easy to add a little glamour to your gingerbread family. Simply leave the dried sugar paste buttons on the prepared tray and brush each one with a little edible glue. Dip the end of a teaspoon in edible glitter, then holding the spoon in one hand, gently tap the handle with the other to lightly dust the buttons with glitter. (For tips on dusting decorations with glitter see page 45). Repeat until all of the buttons are glittered. Tip any excess glitter on the baking parchment back into the pot. Wait until the edible glue is completely dry before attaching the sugar paste buttons as above.

(a)

(b)

Basic Biscuits

**MAKES ABOUT
30 BISCUITS**
250g/9oz salted butter, softened
**200g/7oz/scant 1 cup caster
sugar**
1 large egg, lightly beaten
**450g/1lb/scant 3⅔ cups plain
flour**

YOU WILL NEED
electric mixer
rolling pin
palette knife
**2 baking sheets lined
with baking parchment**

1 Put the butter and sugar in a mixing bowl and beat with the electric mixer until the mixture is just pale and fluffy. Add the egg and beat until combined. Sift the flour into the bowl and mix with a wooden spoon until just combined.

2 Preheat the oven to 180°C/350°F/Gas 4. Roll out the biscuit dough and cut out your biscuits following the instructions on page 148. Tightly wrap any leftover dough in cling film and store in the fridge for up to 1 week or freeze for up to 3 months. Using the palette knife, transfer the biscuits to the prepared baking sheets, spacing them 3cm/1¼in apart to allow each one to spread slightly during cooking.

3 Bake the biscuits for 8 minutes or until golden brown, then remove from the oven. Using the palette knife, transfer the biscuits to a wire cooling rack and leave to cool completely. If not decorating the biscuits immediately, store in an airtight container until needed.

Variations
Almond Biscuits: beat in 1 tsp almond extract with the butter and sugar.
Chocolate Biscuits: use 375g/13oz/3 cups flour and add 75g/2¾oz/scant ⅔ cup cocoa powder.
Citrus Biscuits: beat in the finely grated zest of 1 lemon or 1 orange with the butter and sugar.
Vanilla Biscuits: beat in 1 tsp vanilla extract with the butter and sugar.

Use this biscuit recipe for the following recipes throughout this book:

Kissing Birds Biscuits
page 42

Glitter Filigree Biscuits
page 45

Corset Biscuits
page 50

**Wedding Favour
Blossom Biscuits**
page 58

Rose Heart Biscuits
page 64

**Christmas Wreath
Tree Decorations**
page 72

Thanksgiving Biscuits
page 83

Easter Hen Biscuits
page 99

Mother's Day Biscuits
page 100

Gingerbread Biscuits

**MAKES ABOUT
20 BISCUITS**
100g/3½oz/½ cup soft brown
　sugar
2 tbsp plus 1½ tsp golden syrup
2 tbsp treacle
2 tbsp ground ginger
2 tbsp ground cinnamon
125g/4½oz salted butter, chilled
　and diced
½ tsp bicarbonate of soda
280g/10oz/2¼ cups plain flour

YOU WILL NEED
rolling pin
palette knife
2 baking sheets lined
　with baking parchment

1 Put the sugar, golden syrup, treacle, ginger, cinnamon and 2 tablespoons water in a saucepan. Bring to the boil slowly over a medium-high heat, stirring occasionally, until the mixture is gently bubbling. Remove the pan from the heat and add the butter. Stir until the butter has melted and the mixture is glossy and smooth, then stir in the bicarbonate of soda. Pour the mixture into a large bowl and leave to cool for 30 minutes. When the mixture has cooled, sift the flour into the bowl and mix with a wooden spoon until just combined.

2 Preheat the oven to 180°C/350°F/Gas 4. Roll out the gingerbread dough and cut out your biscuits, following the instructions on page 148. Tightly wrap any leftover dough in cling film and store in the fridge for up to 1 week or freeze for up to 3 months. Using the palette knife, transfer the biscuits to the prepared baking sheets, spacing them 3cm/1¼in apart to allow each one to spread slightly during cooking.

3 Bake the biscuits for 8 minutes or until the edges of the biscuits have darkened slightly, then remove from the oven. Using the palette knife, transfer the biscuits to a wire cooling rack and leave to cool completely. If not decorating the biscuits immediately, store in an airtight container until needed.

Use this gingerbread biscuit recipe for the following recipes throughout this book:

 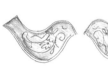   

Gingerbread Family
page 25

Kissing Birds Biscuits
page 42

**Glitter Filigree
Biscuits**
page 45

Corset Biscuits
page 50

**Wedding Favour
Blossom Biscuits**
page 58

Rose Heart Biscuits
page 64

**Christmas Wreath
Tree Decorations**
page 72

Gingerbread House
page 78

Thanksgiving Biscuits
page 83

Easter Hen Biscuits
page 99

Mother's Day Biscuits
page 100

Designer Mini Brownies

**MAKES 30 MINI
BROWNIES**
200g/7oz salted butter, diced
150g/5½oz dark chocolate
50g/1¾oz milk chocolate
375g/13oz/1⅔ cups caster
  sugar
3 large eggs
½ tsp vanilla extract
125g/4½oz/1 cup plain flour
½ tsp baking powder
200g/7oz plain chocolate candy
  coating
chocolate transfer sheet

YOU WILL NEED
25 x 30cm/10 x 12in baking tin
  lined with baking parchment,
  plus extra baking parchment
  for lining the transfer sheet
  (for tips on lining baking tins,
  see page 149)
ruler
palette knife
sharp knife

TIP
Chocolate transfer sheets are
acetate sheets embossed with
cocoa butter and powdered food
colouring. When melted chocolate
is spread on top and left to set,
the design is transferred onto the
surface of the chocolate. Many
different designs are available
online. For beginners, it's easier
to transfer designs onto melted
chocolate candy coating, which
does not need to be tempered
and is also available in dark, milk
and white chocolate flavours.
Heating and cooling chocolate
without controlling the
temperature (tempering) causes
blemishes to appear on the
surface. The chocolate will also
crumble rather than snap.
If you're a confident baker and
decorator, try transferring the
design onto tempered chocolate.

1 Preheat the oven to 180°C/350°F/Gas 4. Melt the butter, dark chocolate and milk chocolate in a large saucepan over a low heat, then remove the pan from the heat. Stir in the sugar, then gradually beat in the eggs, one at a time. Stir in the vanilla extract, then sift the flour and baking powder into the bowl. Fold the flour and baking powder into the mixture with a metal spoon until thoroughly combined and smooth.

2 Pour the mixture into the prepared tin, levelling the surface with the back of a spoon. Bake for 30–35 minutes or until the surface is cracked and a skewer inserted into the centre comes out clean. Take care not to overcook the brownies or they will dry out and loose their soft, dense centres. Remove from the oven and leave in the tin to cool completely.

3 To give your brownies a designer finish, put 175g/6oz of the candy coating in a heatproof bowl and rest it over a saucepan of gently simmering water, making sure the bottom of the bowl does not touch the water. Heat, stirring occasionally, until melted. Alternatively, put the candy coating in a microwavable bowl and microwave, uncovered, on medium for 2 minutes until melted, stirring every 30 seconds to ensure the coating does not overheat. The candy coating should have a smooth pouring consistency similar to double cream.

4 Cut the chocolate transfer sheet into a 25 x 30cm/10 x 12in rectangle, then cut out a sheet of baking parchment or foil that is slightly larger than the transfer sheet. Put the sheet of baking parchment on the work surface and lay the chocolate transfer sheet, embossed-side up, over the top. Spoon the melted candy coating onto the transfer sheet and use the palette knife to spread it into as thin and even a layer as possible. Leave to semi-set for about 5 minutes, until the surface of the candy coating loses its shiny appearance.

5 Using the sharp knife, cut through the candy coating and transfer sheet to form thirty 5 x 5cm/2 x 2in squares. If you find the knife is dragging through the candy coating as you cut, leave it to set for another minute or so, then try again. Carefully put the candy-coated transfer sheet squares in the fridge and leave to chill for 20 minutes or until the candy coating has completely set. Make sure that the squares are kept flat.

6 Meanwhile, cut the brownies into thirty 5 x 5cm/2 x 2in squares. When the transfer sheet squares have completely set, use the sharp knife to gently ease the squares away from the acetate. Melt the remaining candy coating as above in step 3. Spread a little melted candy coating over the surface of each brownie and place a transfer sheet decoration over the top.

Chocolate Fan Cake

MAKES 1 CAKE
icing sugar, for dusting
20g/¾oz milk modelling
chocolate
20g/¾oz dark modelling
chocolate
2 x 15cm/6in round Rich
Chocolate Cakes (see pages
56–7)
½ recipe quantity Chocolate
Buttercream (see page 16)
½ recipe quantity Chocolate
Ganache (see page 16)

YOU WILL NEED
small rolling pin
sharp knife
ruler
tray lined with baking
parchment
15cm/6in round cake drum

TIP
Using a palette knife to cover the
cake with ganache will produce an
attractive textured finish.

1 Dust the work surface with a little icing sugar, then knead the milk modelling chocolate until it is soft and pliable. Roll out the kneaded modelling chocolate quite thinly and cut out 3 rectangles, each about 5 x 9cm/2 x 3½in **(a)**, re-rolling the modelling paste for the third rectangle, if necessary.

2 Gently concertina each rectangle, pinching the folds together at the base to form a fan **(b)**. Using the sharp knife, cut off any excess modelling chocolate at the base of the fans to neaten the edges **(c)**. Repeat steps 1 and 2 with the dark modelling chocolate to make six fans in total. Transfer the fans to the prepared tray and leave to set for a few hours or overnight, uncovered, in a cool, dry place.

3 When the fans have dried, following the instructions on page 150 and using the cake drum as a firm base, layer the chocolate cakes, then fill them with chocolate buttercream to make one tall cake. Following the instructions on page 152, cover the cake with chocolate ganache. Chill in the fridge for 2 hours.

4 When the ganache has set, arrange the chocolate fans on top of the cake, gently pressing them into the ganache to hold them in place.

(a)

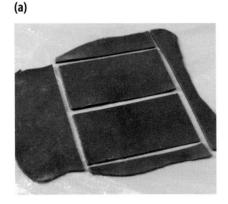

(b)

(c)

Decadent Fruit Tarts

MAKES 12 TARTS
40g/1½oz caramel sugar paste (see pages 160–1)
60g/2¼oz/½ cup icing sugar, sifted, plus extra for dusting
30g/1oz/scant ⅓ cup ground almonds
100g/3½oz chilled salted butter, diced, plus extra for greasing
190g/6¾oz/heaped 1½ cups plain flour
5 large egg yolks
60g/2¼oz/heaped ¼ cup caster sugar
¼ tsp vanilla extract
265ml/9½fl oz/generous 1 cup whole milk
gold edible lustre dust
200g/7oz fresh fruit, such as raspberries, blueberries and blackberries

YOU WILL NEED
rolling pin
2.5cm/1in veined leaf plunger cutter
indented foam pad or a piece of crinkled kitchen foil
12-cup muffin tin
baking parchment
5mm/¼in marzipan spacers (optional)
8.5cm/3½in fluted or plain pastry cutter
ceramic baking beans or rice
small paintbrush
piping bag

TIP
Make the gold sugar paste leaves at least a day before they are needed.

1 Dust the work surface with a little icing sugar, then knead the caramel sugar paste until it is soft and pliable. Roll out the kneaded sugar paste quite thinly and stamp out a leaf using the 2.5cm/1in veined leaf plunger cutter. While the sugar paste is still soft, mould the leaf into a slightly curved shape. Stamping and moulding one leaf at a time, repeat with the remaining sugar paste to make 12 leaves in total. Place the leaves on the indented foam pad – this will help the leaves to keep their curved shape as they dry. Leave the leaves to dry overnight, uncovered, in a cool, dry place.

2 The next day, put the icing sugar, ground almonds, butter and 170g/6oz/heaped 1⅓ cups of the flour in a food processor and pulse for about 15 seconds until the mixture resembles coarse breadcrumbs. Add 1 of the egg yolks and pulse until the mixture just comes together to form a dough. If the dough is too dry, gradually add 1–2 tablespoons of cold water, one tablespoon at a time. Shape the dough into a ball, handling it as little as possible. Wrap in cling film and chill in the fridge for at least 30 minutes.

3 Preheat the oven to 180°C/350°F/Gas 4 and lightly grease the muffin tin with butter. Unwrap the dough and turn it out onto a sheet of baking parchment lightly dusted with icing sugar, then lay another sheet of baking parchment over the top. Roll out the dough between the two sheets until it is about 5mm/¼in thick, using marzipan spacers if you like. Cut out 12 pastry circles with the 8.5cm/3½in circle cutter, then gently press them into the prepared muffin cups.

4 Cut out 12 squares of baking parchment, each large enough to cover a pastry case. Prick each pastry case a few times with a fork, then line with a square of baking parchment and fill with baking beans. Blind bake the pastry cases for 15 minutes or until golden brown. Remove from the oven and leave in the tin to cool a little, then gently ease the pastry cases out of the tin and transfer to a wire rack. Leave to cool completely.

5 To make the crème pâtissière, put the remaining egg yolks, 30g/1oz of the caster sugar and the vanilla extract in a large mixing bowl and whisk until pale. Sift in the remaining flour and whisk until combined. Put the milk and the remaining caster sugar in a saucepan over a medium-low heat and bring just to the boil. Remove from the heat and leave to cool for 1 minute. Gradually pour the hot milk into the egg mixture, whisking continuously. Return the mixture to the saucepan and return to the boil over a medium-low heat, stirring constantly, for 5 minutes until thick and glossy. Pour the crème pâtissière into a clean bowl and cover with cling film, making sure the film touches the surface of the crème pâtissière – this prevents a skin forming. Leave to cool completely. Meanwhile, put a little gold edible lustre dust in a small bowl. Add water, a few drops at a time, and mix until a thick paint forms. Paint the sugar paste leaves with the lustre paint and leave to dry completely. When the leaves have dried and the crème pâtissière has cooled, spoon the crème pâtissière into the piping bag, then snip off the tip if necessary. Pipe a layer of crème pâtissière in each pastry case, add a layer of fruit and decorate with gold leaves and a dusting of icing sugar.

Raspberry Dust Macarons

MAKES 30 MACARONS
3 large egg whites
60g/2¼oz/heaped ¼ cup caster
   sugar
pink food colouring paste
150g/5½oz/1¼ cups icing sugar
100g/3½oz/1 cup ground
   almonds
20g/¾oz dried raspberry
   powder
150g/5½oz/scant ½ cup
   seedless raspberry jam

YOU WILL NEED
electric mixer
cocktail sticks
2 baking sheets
4 piping guide templates
   (see page 170)
baking parchment
piping bag fitted with a
   10mm/½in plain nozzle
small offset palette knife

1 Put the egg whites in a mixing bowl and beat with the electric mixer for 2 minutes until they just start to form soft peaks – if your egg whites are very fresh you may have to beat for a little longer. With the mixer running, gradually add the sugar and continue to beat until the mixture is thick and glossy but not too stiff. Add a small amount of pink food colouring paste to the mixture, using the end of a cocktail stick, and gently whisk until combined. Repeat until the desired colour is achieved, bearing in mind that the colour of the mixture will fade slightly when baked.

2 Sift the icing sugar and ground almonds into a separate mixing bowl. Add one-third of the pink meringue mixture and gently fold it into the icing sugar and ground almonds until incorporated. Add the remaining pink meringue mixture and fold until completely incorporated.

3 Using a spatula, press and spread the mixture up the side of the bowl. Repeat this about ten times, letting the mixture drop back down into the bowl, until the macaron mixture is smooth and has a slow-dripping consistency – this process helps to give the macarons their shine once baked.

4 Take the baking sheets and lay 2 piping guides over each one, then lay a sheet of baking parchment over the top of the guides. Spoon the macaron mixture into the piping bag. Using the guides as a template, pipe out 60 large dots of macaron mixture onto the baking sheets – take care not to pipe outside the circle outlines on the guides as the mixture will spread a little once piped. (For tips on piping, see pages 157–9.) Carefully slide the piping guides off the baking sheets, leaving the baking parchment in place.

5 Sharply tap the baking sheets on the work surface a few times to remove any air bubbles from the macarons – this also helps to smooth the mixture and create a frilly "foot". Lightly sprinkle the dried raspberry powder over the top of 30 of the macarons with a teaspoon. Leave the macarons, uncovered, in a cool, dry place until a very light crust forms over the top of each one and they are dry to the touch – this should take about 15–45 minutes depending on room temperature and humidity. Meanwhile, preheat the oven to 140°C/275°F/Gas 1.

6 Bake the macarons for 13–15 minutes or until the macarons can be lifted cleanly off the baking parchment with the offset palette knife. Remove from the oven and, without removing the macarons, slide the sheets of baking parchment onto wire racks and leave to cool completely.

7 When the macarons have cooled, carefully remove them from the baking parchment with the offset palette knife. Spoon 1 teaspoon of jam onto the flat-sides of the plain macarons, taking care to spoon the jam into the centre to prevent it from spreading out over the side when you sandwich the macarons together. Sandwich together the jam-covered halves with the raspberry-dusted halves to make 30 filled macarons in total.

Chocolate-Dipped Florentines

MAKES 8 FLORENTINES
20g/¾oz salted butter
70g/2½oz/scant ⅓ cup golden
  caster sugar
3 tbsp double cream
1 heaped tbsp plain flour
60g/2¼oz flaked almonds
60g/2¼oz preserved stem
  ginger in syrup, drained and
  finely chopped
finely grated zest of 1 orange
150g/5½oz dark or milk
  chocolate, or half of each

YOU WILL NEED
20 x 20cm/8 x 8in baking tin
  lined with baking parchment
  (for tips on lining baking tins,
  see page 149)
sharp knife
tray lined with baking
  parchment

1 Preheat the oven to 180°C/350°F/Gas 4. Put the butter, sugar and cream in a saucepan and heat, stirring continuously, over a medium heat until the butter has melted and the sugar has dissolved. Stir in the flour, then add the almonds, stem ginger and orange zest and cook, stirring continuously, until thoroughly combined. Remove the pan from the heat.

2 Spoon the mixture into the prepared baking tin, then level with a metal spoon. Bake for 13 minutes or until golden brown. Remove from the oven and leave to cool in the tin for 5 minutes. Without removing the baking parchment, remove the florentine from the tin and place on a flat surface. While it is still warm, cut the florentine into 8 fingers with the sharp knife. Transfer the fingers to a wire rack and leave to cool completely.

3 Put the chocolate in a heatproof bowl and rest it over a saucepan of gently simmering water, making sure the bottom of the bowl does not touch the water. Heat, stirring occasionally, until melted. Alternatively, put the chocolate in a microwavable bowl and microwave, uncovered, on medium for 2 minutes until melted, stirring every 30 seconds to ensure the chocolate does not burn.

4 Dip the end of each florentine finger into the melted chocolate, then transfer them to the prepared tray. Leave the florentines for at least 10–15 minutes, uncovered, in a cool, dry place to allow the chocolate to set.

Marble Swirl Mini Meringues

MAKES 30 MERINGUES
2 large egg whites
115g/4oz/½ cup caster sugar
2 tsp rosewater
pink food colouring paste

YOU WILL NEED
2 baking sheets
2 piping guide templates
 (see page 170)
baking parchment
electric mixer
baking tin
piping bag fitted with a
 10mm/½in plain nozzle
small offset palette knife

1 Preheat the oven to 110°C/225°F/Gas ½. Take the baking sheets and lay a piping guide over each one, then lay a sheet of baking parchment over the top of each guide. Put the egg whites in a mixing bowl and beat with the electric mixer until they start to form soft peaks. With the mixer running, gradually add the sugar and continue to beat until the mixture is thick and glossy. Gently stir in the rosewater.

2 Pour the meringue mixture into the baking tin, roughly spreading it out over the bottom of the tin. Using a fork, dot the meringue mixture with a little pink food colouring paste, then drag the fork through the mixture to create a marbled pattern **(a)**, bearing in mind that the colour of the mixture will fade slightly when baked.

3 Gently spoon the meringue mixture into the piping bag, taking care to keep the marbled pattern intact **(b)** – this will maximize the marbled effect when piping. Using the guides as a template, pipe out 30 meringue swirls onto the baking sheets, starting from the edge of the circles and swirling towards the centre **(c)**. (For tips on piping, see pages 157–9.) Carefully slide the piping guides off the baking sheets, leaving the baking parchment in place.

4 Bake for 45–60 minutes or until the meringues can be lifted cleanly off the baking parchment with the offset palette knife. If the meringues stick to the parchment, bake for a further 10–15 minutes before testing again. When the meringues are ready, turn off the oven and open the door slightly. Leave the meringues in the cooling oven for 20 minutes, then remove and carefully lift each one off the baking parchment with the offset palette knife. Leave to cool completely.

(a)

(b)

(c)

CHAPTER TWO

Certain occasions provide the perfect excuse to treat our loved ones. Whether it's with a Chocolate Heart Cake Pop on Valentine's Day to say "I love you"; a batch of Wedding Favour Blossom Biscuits to say "Thank you for sharing our special day"; or a cake topped with handmade truffles to celebrate that milestone anniversary, you'll create wonderful memories.

DECORATE
FOR
LOVE

Kissing Birds Biscuits

**MAKES 30 BISCUITS
(15 PAIRS)**
icing sugar, for dusting
**200g/7oz bright pink-coloured
sugar paste (see pages 160–1)**
**150g/5½oz white stiff-peak
Royal Icing (see page 46)**
**30 biscuits made using
1 recipe quantity Biscuit
Dough of your choice (see
pages 26–7) cut out with
a bird biscuit cutter**
**edible glue or 35g/1¼oz
apricot jam, warmed**

YOU WILL NEED
small rolling pin
small culinary stencil
small offset palette knife
bird biscuit cutter
small paintbrush
**small piping bag fitted
with a no. 2 plain nozzle**

TIP
To make the birds in "kissing"
pairs, cut out half the birds facing
right and half facing left. To
achieve a mirrored stencil design
on the facing birds, simply turn
the stencil over before you place
it on top of the sugar paste.

1 Dust the work surface with a little icing sugar, then take about 20g/¾oz of the sugar paste and knead until it is soft and pliable. Keep the remaining sugar paste in an airtight container until needed so it does not dry out and crack. Roll out the kneaded sugar paste quite thinly.

2 Place your stencil in the centre of the sugar paste and lightly hold it in place with one hand – if the stencil moves, the design may smudge. Using the offset palette knife, spread a little royal icing over the stencil **(a)**. Remove any excess royal icing with the palette knife, then carefully peel away the stencil.

3 Immediately position the bird biscuit cutter over the stencilled design **(b)**. When you're happy with the effect, cut out a bird from the sugar paste. Roll the trimmings into a ball and add to the remaining sugar paste. Brush the surface of one of the biscuits with edible glue. Clean the offset palette knife, then place the sugar paste bird over the prepared biscuit, taking care not to stretch the sugar paste. Decorating one biscuit at a time and dusting the work surface with icing sugar as necessary, repeat with the remaining sugar paste, royal icing, biscuits and edible glue to make 30 iced biscuits in total. Remember to wash and dry the stencil thoroughly before decorating each biscuit.

4 To finish, spoon the remaining royal icing into the piping bag and pipe a closed eye onto the face of each bird (see picture). (For tips on piping, see pages 157–9.) Leave the biscuits for at least 1 hour, uncovered, in a cool, dry place to allow the icing to set.

(a)

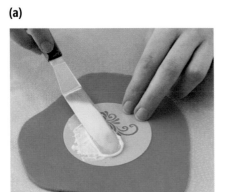

(b)

Glitter Filigree Biscuits

MAKES 12 BISCUITS
12 biscuits made using ½ recipe quantity Biscuit Dough of your choice (see pages 26–7), cut out with the heart template (see page 162) or with a heart biscuit cutter, just baked
70g/2½oz purple-coloured soft-peak Royal Icing (see page 46)
purple, white and gold edible glitters
70g/2½oz white soft-peak Royal Icing (see page 46)
70g/2½oz caramel-coloured soft-peak Royal Icing (see page 46)

YOU WILL NEED
5mm/¼in circle cutter (optional)
baking parchment
3 piping bags, each fitted with a no. 2 plain nozzle
small paintbrush
3 x 1m/39in purple, ivory and gold ribbons, 5mm/¼in wide, each cut into 4 equal pieces (optional)
cocktail stick, if needed

TIP
Use different food colouring pastes, edible glitters and ribbons to create your own colour scheme.

1 As soon as the biscuits come out of the oven, carefully stamp out a small hole at the top of each one with the 5mm/¼in circle cutter or with the end of a drinking straw while they are still hot, then transfer to a wire rack and leave to cool completely.

2 When the biscuits have cooled, lay three sheets of baking parchment on the work surface and place 4 biscuits on each one. Spoon the purple soft-peak royal icing into one of the piping bags. Decorating one biscuit at a time and using the picture as a guide, pipe a heart outline around the biscuit, then pipe the filigree design using curvy lines and dots **(a)**. Dip the end of a teaspoon into the purple edible glitter, then, holding the spoon in one hand, gently tap the handle with the other to lightly dust the icing with glitter **(b)**. Working in colour batches, repeat step 2 continuing to ice and glitter one biscuit at a time to make 12 iced biscuits in total, then leave for at least 1 hour, uncovered, in a cool, dry place to allow the icing to set.

3 When the icing has completely set, gently remove any excess glitter from the biscuits with a paintbrush and tip any excess glitter on the sheets of baking parchment back into their pots. Take a length of purple ribbon and carefully thread it through the hole of a biscuit with purple icing, using the cocktail stick to help push the ribbon through the hole if necessary, then finish with a bow, if you like. Repeat with the remaining biscuits and ribbons to make 12 finished biscuits.

(a)

(b)

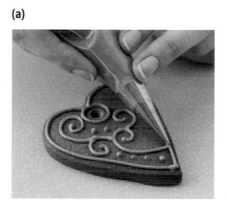

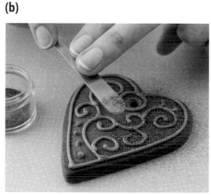

Royal Icing

**MAKES ABOUT
600G/1LB 5OZ**
**2 tbsp pasteurized dried egg
white powder or 2 large
egg whites**
500g/1lb 2oz/4 cups icing sugar
squeeze of lemon juice
food colouring pastes (optional)

YOU WILL NEED
electric mixer
cocktail stick (optional)

TIP
Royal icing can be stored for up
to 7 days in an airtight container
in the fridge. The icing may split
during storage, so make sure you
whisk it thoroughly before use.

Depending on its purpose, royal icing is made up to one of three consistencies: stiff-peak, soft-peak and flood-consistency. It can be coloured any shade you want. Simply add a small amount of food colouring paste to the icing using the end of a cocktail stick, and mix until combined. Repeat until the desired colour is achieved. (For extra tips on consistency, and for tips on piping intricate details, see page 159.)

Stiff-Peak Royal Icing

Stiff-peak royal icing is traditionally used to ice Christmas and celebration cakes. It is often used to attach large, heavy decorations to cakes or to secure ones that need to be held in a vertical position. It can also be used to attach cakes to cake drums and to secure tiers of a cake during stacking. To make stiff-peak royal icing, put 90ml/3fl oz/⅓ cup boiling water in a small bowl and leave to cool completely. When the water has cooled, add the dried egg-white powder, if using, to the bowl and mix well. Cover with cling film and chill in the fridge for at least a few hours or overnight. Sift the icing sugar into a mixing bowl. Add the reconstituted dried egg whites (or fresh egg whites if using) and lemon juice and beat with the electric mixer until just combined, then beat for 5 minutes until the mixture forms stiff peaks. Immediately transfer to an airtight container.

Soft-Peak Royal Icing

Soft-peak royal icing is used to pipe outlines onto biscuits before they are flooded (see below). It can also be used to pipe decorative lines and dots onto cakes and biscuits, and to attach smaller, lighter decorations to cakes. To make soft-peak royal icing, make up a batch of stiff-peak royal icing as above, then stir in cold water, a few drops at a time, until the icing slackens a little and forms soft peaks. Immediately transfer to an airtight container.

Flood-Consistency Royal Icing

Flood-consistency royal icing is used to fill or "flood" the middle of biscuits outlined with soft-peak royal icing. To make flood-consistency royal icing, make up a batch of stiff-peak royal icing as above, then stir in cold water, a few drops at a time, until the icing slackens completely and has a smooth pouring consistency similar to double cream. Immediately transfer to an airtight container.

Use this royal icing recipe for the following recipes throughout this book:

Gingerbread Family
page 25

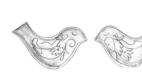

Kissing Birds Biscuits
page 42

Glitter Filigree Biscuits
page 45

Corset Biscuits
page 50

**Chocolate Box
Cake with Truffles**
page 52

**Wedding Favour
Blossom Biscuits**
page 58

**Christmas Wreath
Tree Decorations**
page 72

Gingerbread House
page 78

Thanksgiving Biscuits
page 83

**White Blossom
Christening Cake**
page 84

Festive Ball Cakes
page 92

Easter Hen Biscuits
page 99

**Birthday Butterfly
Mini Domes**
page 104

Santa's Sleigh Cake
page 107

**Ivory Corsage
Wedding Cake**
page 114

Butterfly Fancies
page 116

**Magnificent
Mini Cakes**
page 121

Teapot Cake
page 122

Hydrangea Cake
page 130

Flower Cake Pops
page 132

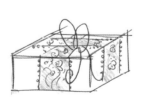

Gift-Wrapped Cake
page 135

Valentine Cigarillo Cake

MAKES 1 CAKE
2 x 15cm/6in round Marble Cakes (see pages 76–7)
1 recipe quantity Vanilla Buttercream (see page 16)
70 x 10cm/4in white chocolate cigarillos
200g/7oz white chocolate drops
400g/14oz strawberries at room temperature

YOU WILL NEED
15cm/6in round cake card
1m/39in pale pink chiffon ribbon, 4cm/1½in wide (optional)
tray lined with baking parchment

TIPS
Chocolate cigarillos are widely available online. For larger round cakes you will need:
80 cigarillos for 18cm/7in
90 cigarillos for 20cm/8in
100 cigarillos for 23cm/9in
110 cigarillos for 25cm/10in

Heating and cooling chocolate without controlling the temperature (tempering) causes blemishes to appear on the surface. The chocolate will also crumble rather than snap. Adding unmelted chocolate to melted chocolate (see step 3) is a simple and easy way to temper chocolate.

1 Following the instructions on page 150 and using the cake card as a base, layer the cakes, then fill with buttercream to make one tall cake. Following the instructions on page 152, cover the cake with the remaining buttercream. The cake should be no taller than 7.5cm/3in – if it is too high the cigarillos will not rise above the cake and the chocolate-dipped strawberries will fall off the top. Chill the cake in the fridge for 2 hours.

2 When the buttercream has set, gently press the cigarillos vertically into the side of the cake, making sure they are as straight as possible and squarely lined up at the base **(a)** – the buttercream will hold them in position. Hold the cigarillos as lightly as possible to prevent them from melting. Tie the ribbon around the cake and finish with a bow, if you like.

3 Put half of the white chocolate drops in a heatproof bowl and rest it over a saucepan of gently simmering water, making sure the bottom of the bowl does not touch the water. Heat, stirring occasionally, until melted. Alternatively, put the chocolate drops in a microwavable bowl and microwave, uncovered, on medium for 2 minutes until melted, stirring every 30 seconds to ensure the chocolate does not burn. Remove the pan from the heat and add the remaining chocolate drops, stirring until the drops have melted and the mixture has thickened slightly.

4 Holding them by the stalks, dip the tip of each strawberry into the melted chocolate. Lift the strawberries out of the coating, allowing any excess chocolate to fall back into the bowl, then transfer them to the prepared tray. Leave the coated strawberries for at least 10–15 minutes, uncovered, at room temperature to allow the chocolate to set. Do not chill the strawberries in the fridge.

5 When the chocolate has set, pile the chocolate-dipped strawberries on top of the cake and eat within 1 day.

(a)

Corset Biscuits

MAKES 12 BISCUITS
240g/8½oz pale pink-coloured
soft-peak Royal Icing
(see page 46)
12 biscuits made using ½ recipe
quantity Biscuit Dough of your
choice (see pages 26–7), cut
out with the corset template
(see page 162)
60g/2¼oz white soft-peak Royal
Icing (see page 46)

YOU WILL NEED
piping bag fitted with a no. 2
plain nozzle
squeeze icing bottle
piping bag fitted with a no. 1.5
plain nozzle

TIP
For a more dramatic look, outline
and flood the biscuit with red
icing and use black icing for the
corset detail.

1 Spoon the pale pink soft-peak royal icing into the piping bag fitted with the no. 2 plain nozzle.
Pipe a corset outline onto each biscuit **(a)**. (For tips on piping, see pages 157–9.) Leave the biscuits
for at least 10–15 minutes, uncovered, in a cool, dry place to allow the icing to set.

2 Spoon the remaining pale pink soft-peak royal icing into a bowl and add enough water to slacken
it to flood consistency (see page 46). Pour the flood icing into the icing bottle and flood the centre
of each biscuit **(b)**. Leave the biscuits for at least 1 hour, uncovered, in a cool, dry place to allow the
icing to set.

3 When the icing has set, spoon the white soft-peak royal icing into the piping bag fitted with the
no. 1.5 plain nozzle. Decorating one biscuit at a time and using the picture as a guide, pipe the white
lace detail over each biscuit **(c)**. Leave the biscuits overnight, uncovered, in a cool, dry place to allow
the icing to set completely.

(a)

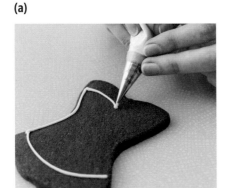

(b)

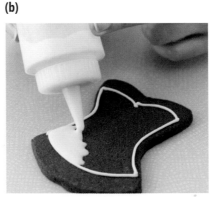

(c)

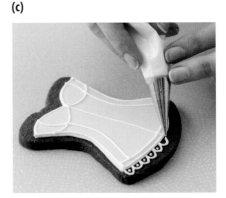

Chocolate Box Cake with Truffles

MAKES 25 TRUFFLES
**400g/14oz dark chocolate, 70%
   cocoa solids, broken into small
   pieces**
**200ml/7fl oz/scant 1 cup double
   cream**
50g/1¾oz/scant ½ cup icing sugar
**cocoa powder, for dusting
   (optional)**

YOU WILL NEED
**3.5cm/1⅓in spring-action-
   release ice cream scoop
   (optional)**
**tray lined with baking
   parchment**
chocolate dipping fork (optional)

TIP
If the mixture splits, warm up a
little more cream, add it to the
mixture and stir until smooth.

TRUFFLES

1 Put 250g/9oz of the chocolate in a heatproof bowl. Pour the cream into a small saucepan and bring just to the boil over a medium-low heat. Pour the cream over the chocolate in the bowl **(a)** and leave to stand for 5 minutes until the chocolate has melted **(b)**. Make sure to stir occasionally, but take care not to overmix or the mixture will split. Add the icing sugar and stir until smooth. Leave to cool completely, then chill in the fridge for 1–2 hours until firm.

2 When the mixture is firm, scoop out a walnut-sized piece, using the ice cream scoop or tablespoon **(c)**, then gently roll it into a ball. Transfer the truffle to the prepared tray and repeat with the remaining mixture to make 25–30 truffles. Chill in the fridge until needed.

3 Put the remaining chocolate in a heatproof bowl and rest it over a saucepan of gently simmering water, making sure the bottom of the bowl does not touch the water. Heat, stirring occasionally, until melted. Alternatively, put the chocolate in a microwavable bowl and microwave, uncovered, on medium for 2 minutes until melted, stirring every 30 seconds to ensure the chocolate does not burn.

(a)   **(b)**   **(c)**

(d)   **(e)**   **(f)**

4 Drop one of the truffles into the melted chocolate. Using the chocolate dipping fork or a dinner fork, gently twist the truffle through the chocolate until it is completely coated **(d)**. Lift the truffle out of the coating, allowing any excess chocolate to fall back into the bowl **(e)**. Return the chocolate-coated truffle to the prepared tray, then repeat with the remaining truffles and melted chocolate until all the truffles are coated. Return the tray to the fridge and leave to chill until the coating has set. When set, remove the truffles from the fridge and lightly dust with cocoa powder, if you like **(f)**. Transfer to an airtight container and chill in the fridge until needed.

MAKES 1 FLOWER
icing sugar, for dusting
40g/1½oz pale yellow-coloured
   sugar paste (see pages 160–1)
40g/1½oz white sugar paste
   (see pages 160–1)
edible glue or cooled, boiled
   water

YOU WILL NEED
small rolling pin
sharp knife
small, medium and large flower
   templates (see page 167) or
   3.5cm/1⅓in, 4.5cm/1¾in and
   6cm/2½in flower cutters
foam pad or a clean, dry folded
   kitchen towel
veiner tool
indented foam pad or a piece of
   crinkled foil
small paintbrush

CHOCOLATE BOX

For the Flower

1 Dust the work surface with a little icing sugar, then knead the sugar pastes until they are soft and pliable. Roll out the pale yellow sugar paste quite thinly and cut out a small flower and a large flower using the small and large flower templates. Roll out half of the white sugar paste quite thinly and cut out a medium flower using the medium template. Roll a little of the white sugar paste trimmings into a pea sized ball and set it aside to firm up a little.

2 Place the flowers on the foam pad, then roll the veiner tool over each petal to create a textured effect **(g)**. Place the largest flower on the indented foam pad. Brush a little edible glue in the centre of the largest flower, then lay the medium flower over the top. Repeat using a little more edible glue to attach the small flower to the centre of the medium flower **(h)**. Attach the pea-sized ball of white sugar paste to the centre of the flower with a little edible glue **(i)**. Leave the flower to dry overnight, uncovered, in a cool, dry place.

(g)

(h)

(i)

**MAKES 2 LEAVES,
1 GIFT TAG AND THE
CHOCOLATE BOX**
icing sugar, for dusting
30g/1oz green-coloured sugar
  paste (see pages 160–1)
425g/15oz white sugar paste
  (see pages 160–1)
20cm/8in Rich Chocolate Heart
  Cake (see pages 56–7)
1 recipe quantity Vanilla
  Buttercream (see page 16)
700g/1lb 9oz pale yellow-
  coloured sugar paste (see
  pages 160–1)
50g/1¾oz white soft-peak Royal
  Icing (see page 46)

YOU WILL NEED
rolling pin
sharp knife
leaf template (see page 167)
foam pad or a clean, dry folded
  kitchen towel
veiner tool
ruler
5mm/¼in circle cutter or the
  end of a drinking straw
design wheeler tool with stitch
  head
20cm/8in heart-shaped cake
  drum
5mm/¼in marzipan spacers
  (optional)
20cm/8in heart-shaped cake tin
icing smoother
20cm/8in yellow ribbon,
  10mm/½in wide
piping bag fitted with a no. 2
  plain nozzle

For the Leaves, Gift Tag and Chocolate Box

1 Dust the work surface with a little icing sugar, then knead the green sugar paste and 50g/1¾oz of the white sugar paste until they are soft and pliable. To make the leaves, roll out the green sugar paste quite thinly and cut out 2 leaves using the leaf template. Place the leaves on the foam pad, then roll the veiner tool over the leaves to create a textured effect. Pinch the sugar paste together at the base of the leaves to form an inward curve **(j)**.

2 To make the gift tag, roll out the 50g/1¾oz of the white sugar paste quite thinly and cut out a 8 x 5cm/3¼ x 2in rectangle. Cut one end to a point and stamp out a small hole with the 5mm/¼in circle cutter. Use the design wheeler tool to indent a "stitched" line around the edge of the tag **(k)**. Leave the leaves and gift tag to dry overnight, uncovered, in a cool, dry place.

3 When the decorations have dried, follow the instructions on page 150 and layer the cake, then fill with buttercream. Following the instructions on page 152 and using the cake drum as a firm base, cover the cake with the remaining buttercream. Chill in the fridge for 2 hours until set. When the buttercream has set, dust the work surface with a little icing sugar, then knead the remaining white sugar paste, and the pale yellow sugar paste until they are soft and pliable. Roll out the white sugar paste until it is 5mm/¼in thick, using marzipan spacers if you like. Using the cake tin as a template, cut out a heart shape from the sugar paste. Lay the heart on top of the cake, smoothing it down with your hands and then with the icing smoother.

4 To make the sides of the box, roll out the pale yellow sugar paste until it is 5mm/¼in thick, using marzipan spacers if you like, and cut out a 70 x 7cm/28 x 2¾in rectangle. Attach it to the side of the cake **(l)**, smoothing it down with your hands and then with the icing smoother and trimming as necessary. The rectangle should cover the sides and be tall enough to create a shallow "box" on top of the cake. Attach the ribbon to the gift tag. Spoon the royal icing into the piping bag and pipe a message onto the gift tag if you like, such as "with love", then pipe a polka-dot design around the sides of the cake. (For tips on piping, see pages 157–9). Arrange the truffles in the "box" and top with the decorations, securing them with the remaining royal icing. Allow the icing to set before serving.

(j)

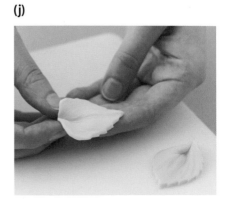

(k)

(l)

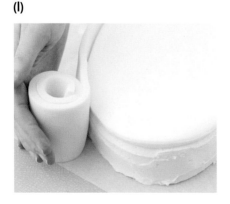

Rich Chocolate Cake

salted butter
dark chocolate, 70% cocoa solids
coffee extract
egg(s)
milk
self-raising flour
plain flour
bicarbonate of soda
cocoa powder
caster sugar

YOU WILL NEED
**cake tin(s) lined with baking
   parchment (for tips on lining
   cake tins, see page 149)**

TIP
If the cake is going to be split
into layers, wrap it in baking
parchment and foil, then leave
it to rest overnight to firm up a
little – this will make it easier to
cut. (For tips on layering, filling
and covering cakes, see pages 150
and 152–3.)

**The table opposite shows you the quantity of ingredients and baking times required
for different cake sizes and styles. It also offers advice on serving portions. Simply
select your size and style and follow the method below.**

1 Preheat the oven to 160°C/315°F/Gas 2–3. Melt the butter and chocolate in a saucepan over a
medium-low heat. Add the coffee extract to the pan and stir until combined, then pour the mixture
into a large mixing bowl.

2 In a jug, lightly beat together the egg(s) and milk. Pour the egg mixture into the chocolate
mixture, stirring to combine. In another bowl, sift together the flours, bicarbonate of soda and cocoa
powder. Gradually add small quantities of the flour mixture to the chocolate mixture, making sure it
is well incorporated before adding more. Add the sugar and stir until combined – the mixture should
be fairly runny by this stage.

3 Spoon the mixture into the prepared cake tin(s), levelling the surface with the back of a spoon.
Bake for the recommended time or until a skewer inserted into the centre comes out clean. As oven
temperatures can vary, check on the cake(s) about 5 minutes before the end of the recommended
baking time.

4 Remove the cake(s) from the oven and leave to cool for 5 minutes, then remove from the tin,
transfer to a wire rack and leave to cool completely.

Use this rich chocolate sponge recipe for the following recipes throughout this book:

Chocolate Fan Cake
page 30

**Chocolate Box Cake
with Truffles**
page 52

Festive Ball Cakes
page 92

Christmas Pudding Cake
page 97

**Ivory Corsage
Wedding Cake**
page 114

	10cm/4in round or square cake 6 cupcakes	13cm/5in round or square cake	15cm/6in round or square cake 4 x 8cm/3¼in mini ball cake halves 24 mini cupcakes	18cm/7in round or square cake	20cm/8in round, square or heart cake 12 cupcakes	23cm/9in round or square cake 2 x 15cm/6in ball cake halves
salted butter	50g/1¾oz	70g/2½oz	100g/3½oz	150g/5½oz	200g/7oz	300g/10½oz
dark chocolate, 70% cocoa solids	25g/1oz	35g/1¼oz	50g/1¾oz	75g/2½oz	100g/3½oz	150g/5½oz
coffee extract	1 tsp	1 tsp	2 tsp	1 tbsp	1 tbsp plus 1 tsp	2 tbsp
eggs	1 medium	1 large	2 medium	2 large	3 large	5 medium
milk	25ml/½fl oz	35ml/1fl oz	50ml/1½fl oz/ 3 tbsp	75ml/2½fl oz/⅓ cup	100ml/3½fl oz/ scant ½ cup	150ml/5fl oz/scant ⅔ cup
self-raising flour	25g/1oz/scant ¼ cup	35g/1¼oz/heaped ¼ cup	50g/1¾oz/scant ½ cup	75g/2½oz/scant ⅔ cup	100g/3½oz/ heaped ¾ cup	150g/5½oz/scant 1¼ cups
plain flour	25g/1oz/scant ¼ cup	35g/1¼oz/heaped ¼ cup	50g/1¾oz/scant ½ cup	75g/2½oz/scant ⅔ cup	100g/3½oz/ heaped ¾ cup	150g/5½oz/scant 1¼ cups
bicarbonate of soda	¼ tsp	¼ tsp	¼ tsp	½ tsp	½ tsp	¾ tsp
cocoa powder	2 tsp	1 tbsp	20g/¾oz/scant ¼ cup	30g/1oz/¼ cup	40g/1½oz/⅓ cup	60g/2¼oz/½ cup
caster sugar	75g/2½oz/scant ⅓ cup	100g/3½oz/scant ½ cup	150g/5½oz/heaped ⅔ cup	225g/8oz/scant 1 cup	300g/10½oz/scant 1⅓ cups	450g/1lb/scant 2 cups
baking time	20 mins for large cakes	25 mins	30 mins for large cakes	40 mins	50 mins for large cakes	1 hour 10 mins for large cakes
	15 mins for cupcakes		15 mins for mini ball cake halves		15 mins for cupcakes	45 mins for ball cake halves
			8 mins for mini cupcakes			
serves	large cakes: 10	12	large cakes: 15–20	20–30	large cakes: 30–40	large cakes: 40–50
	cupcakes: 6		mini ball cake halves: 4		cupcakes: 12	ball cake halves: 12–16
			mini cupcakes: 24			

Wedding Favour Blossom Biscuits

MAKES 30 BISCUITS
150g/5½oz pale blue-coloured soft-peak Royal Icing (see page 46)
30 biscuits made using 1 recipe quantity Biscuit Dough of your choice (see pages 26–7), cut out with the small, medium and large blossom templates (see page 165) to make 10 biscuits of each size
40g/1½oz white pearl effect ball dragees
150g/5½oz ivory-coloured soft-peak Royal Icing (see page 46)

YOU WILL NEED
2 piping bags fitted with no. 2 plain nozzles
2 squeeze icing bottles

TIP
For perfect presentation, transfer the finished biscuits to cellophane gift bags and tie each one with a length of ribbon.

1 Spoon about 60g/2¼oz of the pale blue soft-peak royal icing into one of the piping bags. Pipe a blossom outline around half of the biscuits, then leave for at least 10–15 minutes, uncovered, in a cool, dry place to allow the icing to set. Roll up the piping bag and store in an airtight container until needed. (For tips on piping, see pages 157–9.)

2 Spoon the remaining pale blue soft-peak royal icing into a bowl and add enough water to slacken it to flood consistency (see page 46). Pour the flood icing into one of the icing bottles and flood the centre of one of the biscuits. Before the icing sets, drop a pearl dragee into the centre of the blossom shape. Carefully place another 6 dragees around the central pearl to form a blossom shape. Flooding one biscuit at a time, repeat with the remaining pale blue flood icing, outlined biscuits and dragees to make 15 iced biscuits. Leave the biscuits for at least 1 hour, uncovered, in a cool, dry place to allow the icing to set. Meanwhile, repeat steps 1 and 2 with the ivory soft-peak royal icing and the remaining biscuits and dragees to make 30 iced biscuits in total.

3 When the icing has set, pipe another blossom outline around the edge of each biscuit with the remaining pale blue and ivory soft-peak royal icings. Leave the biscuits overnight, uncovered, in a cool, dry place to allow the icing to completely set.

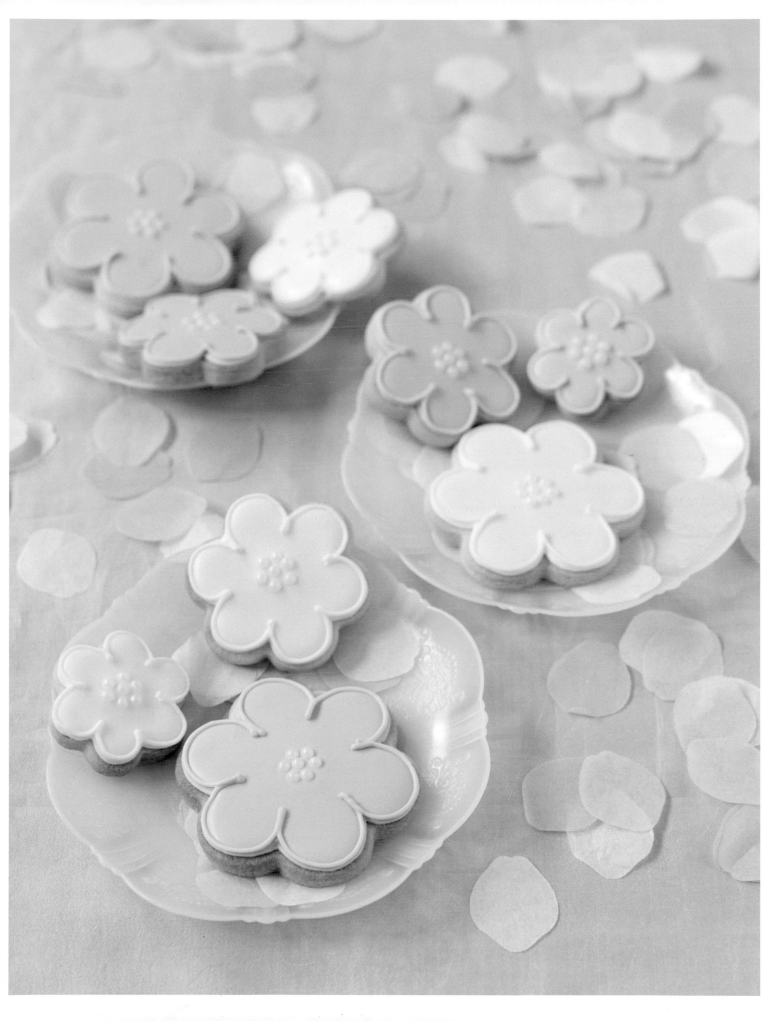

Pom Pom Wedding Cake

MAKES 1 CAKE
2 x 23cm/9in round Vanilla Sponge Cakes (see pages 62–3)
2 x 15cm/6in round Basic Sponge Cakes (see pages 62–3)
2 recipe quantities Vanilla Buttercream (see page 16)
icing sugar, for dusting
1.6kg/3lb 8oz ivory-coloured sugar paste (see pages 160–1)
edible glue or cooled, boiled water
200g/7oz pale pink-coloured sugar paste (pages 160–1)

YOU WILL NEED
23cm/9in round cake drum
15cm/6in round cake drum
plastic dowels
25cm/10in ivory satin ribbon, 25mm/1in wide
small paintbrush
17cm/6½in ivory satin ribbon, 25mm/1in wide
small rolling pin
sharp knife
ruler
1.5cm/⅝in circle cutter
4 sheets of ivory tissue paper
scissors
small length of florist's wire

1 Following the instructions on page 150 and using the cake drums as firm bases, layer the cakes, then fill with buttercream to make one tall 23cm/9in cake and one tall 15cm/6in cake. Following the instructions on page 152, cover the cakes with the remaining buttercream. Chill in the fridge for at least 2 hours. When the buttercream has set, dust the work surface with a little icing sugar, then knead 1kg/2lb 4oz of the ivory sugar paste until it is soft and pliable. Following the instructions on page 153, cover the 23cm/9in cake with the kneaded sugar paste. Repeat with the remaining sugar paste to cover the 15cm/6in cake. Leave the cakes overnight, uncovered, in a cool, dry place to allow the sugar paste to dry. When the sugar paste has dried, follow the instructions on page 156 and stack the 15cm/6in cake on top of 23cm/9in cake with plastic dowels. Wrap the 25cm/10in ribbon around the base of the bottom tier, securing the join at the back with a little edible glue and trimming if necessary, then attach the 17cm/6½in ribbon to the top tier.

2 Dust the work surface with icing sugar, then knead half of the pale pink sugar paste and roll out quite thinly. For the stripes, cut 12 strips of rolled sugar paste, each about 10 x 1.5cm/4 x ⅝in using the sharp knife. Position the strips around the top tier of the cake, making sure they are evenly spaced, as straight as possible and squarely lined up with the ribbon, then secure with edible glue. For the spots, knead the remaining pale pink sugar paste and roll out quite thinly. Stamp out 36 circles with the 1.5cm/⅝in circle cutter. Brush the back of each circle with a little edible glue, then attach the spots to the bottom tier in three rows (see picture).

3 To make the pom pom, lay the sheets of tissue paper one on top of the other and cut out a rectangle about 25 x 15cm/10 x 6in. Crease the paper along the short edge into concertina folds, each about 3cm/1¼in deep. Fold and crease the concertinaed paper in half, then wrap the florist's wire over this central crease **(a)**, twisting to secure and trimming the wire if necessary. Using scissors, round the ends of the paper for a neat finish **(b)**. Separate the layers by gently pulling them apart and upwards to form a dome shape **(c)**, then place the finished pom pom on top of the cake.

(a)

(b)

(c)

Basic Sponge

salted butter
caster sugar
egg(s)
self-raising flour
vanilla extract (optional)
cocoa powder (optional)
lemon or orange zest (optional)
coffee extract (optional)

YOU WILL NEED
electric mixer
cake tin(s) lined with baking
   parchment (for tips on lining
   cake tins, see page 149)

TIP
If the cake is going to be split
into layers, wrap it in baking
parchment and foil, then leave
it to rest overnight to firm up a
little – this will make it easier to
cut (for tips on layering, filling
and covering cakes, see pages
150–153).

The table opposite shows you the quantity of ingredients and baking times required for different cake sizes and styles. It also offers advice on serving portions. Simply select your size and style and follow the method below.

1 Preheat the oven to 180°C/350°F/Gas 4 and allow the butter to soften slightly. Put the sugar and the softened butter in a mixing bowl and beat with the electric mixer for about 3 minutes until light and fluffy. Lightly beat the egg(s), and gradually add to the mixture. If the mixture starts to curdle, add a little bit of the flour. Sift the flour into the bowl and beat until just combined.

2 Spoon the mixture into the prepared cake tin(s), levelling the surface with the back of a spoon. Bake for the recommended time or until the top springs back slightly when gently pressed with a finger and a skewer inserted into the centre comes out clean. As oven temperatures can vary, check on the cake(s) about 5 minutes before the end of the recommended baking time.

3 Remove the cake(s) from the oven and leave to cool for 5 minutes, then remove from the tin, transfer to a wire rack and leave to cool completely.

Flavoured Sponges

Cappuccino Sponge: add coffee extract to the mixture after the eggs have been incorporated (before you add the flour).

Chocolate Sponge: use less self-raising flour and add cocoa powder to the mixture with the flour.

Citrus Sponge: beat in the finely grated zest of lemons or oranges with the sugar and butter.

Mocha Sponge: add coffee extract to the mixture after the eggs have been incorporated. Use less self-raising flour (see chocolate sponge variation for quantity) and add cocoa powder to the mixture with the flour.

Vanilla Sponge: beat in vanilla extract with the sugar and butter.

Use these sponge recipes for the following recipes throughout this book:

**Sugared Rose
Petal Cake**
page 12

**Fresh Flower
Fondant Fancies**
page 18

**Pom Pom
Wedding Cake**
page 60

**Chocolate Heart
Cake Pops**
page 68

Dragon Cake
page 74

**White Blossom
Christening Cake**
page 84

	10cm/4in round or square cake 6 cupcakes	13cm/5in round or square cake	15cm/6in round or square cake 4 x 8cm/3¼in mini ball cake halves 24 mini cupcakes	18cm/7in round or square cake	20cm/8in round, square or heart cake 12 cupcakes	23cm/9in round or square cake 2 x 15cm/6in ball cake halves
salted butter	50g/1¾oz	70g/2½oz	100g/3½oz	150g/5½oz	200g/7oz	300g/10½oz
caster sugar	50g/1¾oz/scant ¼ cup	70g/2½oz/scant ⅓ cup	100g/3½oz/scant ½ cup	150g/5½oz/scant ⅔ cup	200g/7oz/ scant 1 cup	300g/10½oz/ scant 1⅓ cups
eggs	1 medium	1 large	2 large	3 large	4 large	6 large
self-raising flour	50g/1¾oz/ scant ½ cup	70g/2½oz/ heaped ½ cup	100g/3½oz/ heaped ¾ cup	150g/5½oz/ heaped 1¼ cups	200g/7oz/ scant 1⅔ cups	300g/10½oz/ scant 2½ cups
for vanilla sponge	¼ tsp vanilla extract	½ tsp vanilla extract	½ tsp vanilla extract	1 tsp vanilla extract	1 tsp vanilla extract	1½ tsp vanilla extract
for chocolate sponge	1 tsp cocoa powder	2 tsp cocoa powder	2 tsp cocoa powder	1 tbsp cocoa powder	20g/¾oz/scant ¼ cup cocoa powder	40g/1½oz/⅓ cup cocoa powder
	45g/1½oz/heaped ⅓ cup self-raising flour	50g/1¾oz/ scant ½ cup self-raising flour	90g/3¼oz/¾ cup self-raising flour	135g/4¾oz/heaped 1 cup self-raising flour	180g/6¼oz/scant 1½ cups self-raising	260g/9¼oz/scant 2¼ cups self-raising flour
for citrus sponge	zest of ½ lemon or ¼ orange	zest of ½ lemon or ¼ orange	zest of 1 lemon or ½ orange	zest of 2 lemons or 1 orange	zest of 2 lemons or 1 orange	zest of 3 lemons or 1½ oranges
for cappuccino sponge	3 tsp coffee extract	1 tbsp coffee extract	1–2 tbsp coffee extract	2 tbsp coffee extract	3 tbsp coffee extract	5 tbsp coffee extract
for mocha sponge	1 tbsp coffee extract	1 tbsp coffee extract	2 tbsp coffee extract	3 tbsp coffee extract	4 tbsp coffee extract	6 tbsp coffee extract
	1 tsp cocoa powder	1 tsp cocoa powder	2 tsp cocoa powder	1 tbsp cocoa powder	20g/¾oz/scant ¼ cup cocoa powder	30g/1oz/¼ cup cocoa powder
baking time	20 mins for large cakes	25 mins	30 mins for large cakes	35 mins	40 mins for large cakes	50 mins for large cakes
	15 mins for cupcakes		15 mins for mini ball cake halves		12–15 mins for cupcakes	40 mins for ball cake halves
			8 mins for mini cupcakes			
serves	large cakes: 10	12	large cakes: 15–20	20–30	large cakes: 30–40	large cakes: 50–75
	cupcakes: 6		mini ball cake halves: 4		cupcakes: 12	ball cake halves: 12–16
			mini cupcakes: 24			

Festive Ball Cakes
page 92

Christmas Pudding Cake
page 97

Ivory Corsage Wedding Cake
page 114

Butterfly Fancies
page 116

Teapot Cake
page 122

Flower Cake Pops
page 132

Rose Heart Biscuits

MAKES 30 BISCUITS
icing sugar, for dusting
80g/2¾oz pale green-coloured
    sugar paste (see pages 160–1)
80g/2¾oz red-coloured sugar
    paste (see pages 160–1)
edible glue or 30g/1oz white
    Royal Icing (see page 46)
30 biscuits made using 1 recipe
    quantity Biscuit Dough of your
    choice (see pages 26–7), cut
    out with the heart template
    (see page 162) or with a heart
    biscuit cutter

YOU WILL NEED
small rolling pin
2.5cm/1in and 3cm/1¼in veined
    leaf plunger cutters
indented foam pad or a piece of
    crinkled kitchen foil
small single rose mould
small paintbrush
baking sheet, lined with baking
    parchment
small offset palette knife

TIPS
Working in batches will help you
to keep the size of the roses even.

You will need to make the leaves
and the roses the day before they
are needed.

1 To make the leaves, dust the work surface with a little icing sugar, then knead the pale green sugar paste until it is soft and pliable. Roll out the kneaded sugar paste quite thinly and stamp out a leaf using the 2.5cm/1in veined leaf plunger cutter. While the sugar paste is still soft, mould the leaf into a slightly curved shape. Stamping and moulding one leaf at a time **(a)**, repeat with the remaining sugar paste to make 30 leaves in total, using both the 2.5cm/1in and 3cm/1¼in veined leaf plunger cutters to create a mixture of sizes. Place the leaves on the indented foam pad – this will help the leaves to keep their curved shape as they dry. Leave to dry overnight, uncovered, in a cool, dry place.

2 To make the roses, dust the work surface with a little more icing sugar, then knead the red sugar paste until it is soft and pliable. Roll a little of the kneaded sugar paste into 6 pea-sized balls. Keep the remaining sugar paste in an airtight container until needed so it does not dry out and crack. Dust the rose mould with a little icing sugar to prevent the sugar paste from sticking. Gently push one of the sugar paste balls into the mould, applying even pressure with your thumb to ensure the sugar paste picks up all of the detailing **(b)**. Carefully pop the sugar paste rose out of the mould. Remove any excess icing sugar from the rose with the paintbrush, then transfer the rose to the prepared baking sheet with the offset palette knife. Repeat with the remaining balls of red sugar paste to make 6 roses. Working in batches, repeat with the remaining red sugar paste to make 30 roses in total. Leave the roses to dry overnight, uncovered, in a cool, dry place.

3 When the sugar paste decorations have dried, brush the back of the roses and leaves with a little edible glue, then gently press them onto the top of the biscuits to make 30 decorated biscuits. Leave the biscuits for at least 10–15 minutes, uncovered, in a cool, dry place to allow the edible glue to set.

(a)

(b)

Rose Bouquet Cupcakes

MAKES 6 CUPCAKES
icing sugar, for dusting
360g/12¾oz red-coloured sugar paste (see pages 160–1)
edible glue or cooled, boiled water
red edible glitter
½ recipe quantity Chocolate Frosting (see page 118)
6 Rich Chocolate Cupcakes (see page 129), baked in brown cupcake cases

YOU WILL NEED
small rolling pin
sharp knife
ruler
small paintbrush
tray lined with baking parchment
piping bag fitted with a 20mm/¾in closed-star nozzle
6 lengths of red ribbon (optional)

TIPS
You will need to make the roses at least a day before they are needed.

For a softer look, take 6 vanilla cupcakes baked in white cases, cover with high swirls of vanilla buttercream and decorate with pale pink roses. Or, for a jewel-like effect, opt for orange, pink, aqua or lime glittered roses.

1 This recipe makes six cupcakes but if you want to make only one, simply use one-sixth of each of the listed ingredients. Dust the work surface with a little icing sugar, then knead 120g/4¼oz of the sugar paste until it is soft and pliable. Roll out the kneaded sugar paste quite thinly, then cut into strips, each about 1.5 x 6cm/⅝ x 2½in. Roll the trimmings into a ball, then re-roll until quite thin and continue to cut into strips. Repeat until all of the sugar paste is used up.

2 To make a rose, take one of the sugar paste strips and roll the end of the paintbrush along one of the long edges, pressing gently to avoid tearing it, to create the frill at the top of the petals **(a)**. Brush a little water along the three plain edges of the strip. With the frilled-side facing inwards, gently roll up the strip to form a rose **(b)**. Pinch the sugar paste together at the bottom of the rose, then cut off the excess sugar paste to form a flat base. Transfer the finished rose to the prepared tray. Repeat step 2 with the remaining sugar paste strips to make approximately 35 roses. Working in batches, repeat with the remaining sugar paste to make approximately 100 roses in total, dusting the work surface with icing sugar as necessary. Leave the roses to dry overnight, uncovered, in a cool, dry place.

3 When the roses have dried, brush 5–10 roses with a little edible glue. Dip the end of a teaspoon in edible glitter, then holding the spoon in one hand, gently tap the handle with the other to lightly dust the roses with glitter **(c)**. Working in small batches, repeat until all the roses are glittered. Tip any excess glitter on the baking parchment back into the pot.

4 Spoon the chocolate frosting into the piping bag and pipe a high swirl onto one of the cupcakes (see page 157). Arrange 15–16 of the roses in a single layer over the cupcake to cover the frosting. Wrap a length of red ribbon around the base of the cupcake and finish with a bow, if you like. Repeat with the remaining frosting, cupcakes, roses and ribbon, if you like, to make six decorated cupcakes.

(a)

(b)

(c)

Chocolate Heart Cake Pops

MAKES 30 CAKE POPS
20cm/8in Basic Sponge Cake
(see pages 62–3)
¾ recipe quantity Vanilla
Frosting (see page 118)
600g/1lb 5oz chocolate candy
coating

YOU WILL NEED
baking parchment
5cm/2in heart biscuit cutter
30 paper lollipop sticks
6 x 50cm/20in multi-coloured
ribbons, 1cm/½in wide,
each cut into 5 equal lengths
(optional)

TIPS
Making the sponge cake the day before you make the cake pops will make the mixture easier to crumble.

Candy coating is widely available online. You can buy it in various colours and in a variety of flavours, including dark, milk and white chocolate. Candy coating is easy to use because, unlike chocolate, it does not need to be tempered. Heating and cooling chocolate without controlling the temperature (tempering) causes blemishes to appear on the surface. The chocolate will also crumble rather than snap.

1 Put the cake in a mixing bowl and crumble it with your fingers until it resembles coarse breadcrumbs. Make sure there are no large pieces of sponge left in the bowl as this will make the cake pops lumpy. Add the frosting and gently mix to form a moist cake mixture. To test if the mixture is the correct consistency for moulding, take a small amount of mixture and gently press it into a ball shape **(a)** – if the mixture holds its shape, it is ready to use.

2 Lay a sheet of baking parchment on the work surface and place the 5cm/2in heart biscuit cutter on top. Take about 30g/1oz of the cake pop mixture and press it into the cutter to form a smooth base, then use your fingers to mould a smooth, curved front **(b)**. Carefully remove the moulded mixture from the cutter and repeat to make 30 heart-shaped cake pops. Chill the cake pops in the fridge for about 1 hour until firm. Alternatively, freeze the cake pops for about 15 minutes until firm.

3 Put the candy coating in a heatproof bowl and rest it over a saucepan of gently simmering water, making sure the bottom of the bowl does not touch the water. Heat, stirring occasionally, until melted. Alternatively, put the candy coating in a microwavable bowl and microwave, uncovered, on medium for 2 minutes until melted, stirring every 30 seconds to ensure the coating does not overheat. The candy coating should have a smooth pouring consistency similar to double cream.

4 Dip the tip of one of the lollipop sticks about 1cm/½in into the melted candy coating and gently push it into the base of one of the cake pops until the coated tip is hidden from view. Holding the end of the lollipop stick, gently twist the cake pop through the candy coating **(c)** until it is completely coated, using a teaspoon to help if necessary. Lift the cake pop out of the candy coating, allowing any excess coating to fall back into the bowl. Transfer the coated cake pop to a drinking glass, with the cake-pop end upward, and leave to set for 10–15 minutes. Repeat with the remaining cake pops and lollipop sticks, reheating the candy coating if necessary, to make 30 coated cake pops. When the candy coating has completely set, tie a ribbon around each lollipop stick and finish with a bow, if you like.

(a)

(b)

(c)

CHAPTER THREE

Seasonal events and birthdays provide plenty
of opportunities to be creative. My favourite time of year
is undoubtedly Christmas, when baking and decorating can
be even more extravagant than usual. For a spectacular
Christmas centrepiece, try the Gingerbread House or the
Christmas Pudding Cake. If you need to plan an unforgettable
children's birthday party, just invite along the Party Penguins.
Let the celebrations begin!

DECORATE
TO
CELEBRATE

Christmas Wreath Tree Decorations

MAKES 12 BISCUITS

120g/4¼oz green-coloured stiff-peak Royal Icing (see page 46)

12 biscuits made using ¾ recipe quantity Biscuit Dough of your choice (see pages 26–7), cut out with the wreath template (see page 165)

25g/1oz red-coloured stiff-peak Royal Icing (see page 46)

YOU WILL NEED

piping bag fitted with a small leaf nozzle

piping bag fitted with a no. 2 plain nozzle

4m/13ft gold ribbon, 5mm/¼in wide, cut into 24 equal lengths

TIPS

If you don't have a small leaf nozzle, snip a small triangle at the tip of a disposable piping bag to create a similar effect.

To achieve the leaf effect with a piping bag, gently squeeze a small amount of royal icing out of the bag and when the leaf is the correct size, carefully pull the nozzle up and away from the icing. If the leaves are not holding their shape, your royal icing might not be stiff enough. Simply mix in a little more icing sugar before piping again. Repeat if necessary.

1 Spoon the green stiff-peak royal icing into the piping bag fitted with the small leaf nozzle. Decorating one biscuit at a time, pipe rows of leaves over the top of each biscuit – starting from the inside edge and working your way towards the outer edge **(a)**. (For tips on piping, see pages 157–9.) When the biscuit is covered in leaves, pipe a few more leaves over the top to fill any gaps, if necessary. Repeat with the remaining biscuits and green stiff-peak royal icing to make 12 iced biscuits in total. Leave for 15 minutes, uncovered, in a cool, dry place to allow the icing to set.

2 When the icing has set, spoon the red stiff-peak royal icing into the piping bag fitted with the no. 2 plain nozzle. For the berries, pipe tiny dots of red icing over the top of each biscuit. Leave the biscuits overnight, uncovered, in a cool, dry place to allow the icing to set completely.

3 When the icing has completely set, take a length of gold ribbon and carefully thread it through the hole in the biscuit, then tie a bow at the top of the biscuit. Carefully thread another length of ribbon underneath the ribbon at the back of the bow and tie in a loop (see picture). Repeat with the remaining biscuits and ribbons to make 12 hanging tree decorations.

(a)

Dragon Cake

MAKES 1 CAKE
icing sugar, for dusting
150g/5½oz blue-coloured
   modelling paste (see
   pages 160–1)
60g/2¼oz green-coloured
   modelling paste (see
   pages 160–1)
2 x 20cm/8in round Basic
   Sponge Cakes (see pages
   62–3)
1 recipe quantity Vanilla
   Buttercream (see page 16)
100g/3½oz seedless raspberry
   jam
800g/1lb 12oz white sugar paste
   (see pages 160–1)
200g/7oz red-coloured sugar
   paste (see pages 160–1)
edible glue or cooled, boiled
   water
5g/⅛oz black-coloured sugar
   paste (see pages 160–1)

YOU WILL NEED
small rolling pin
5mm/¼in marzipan spacers
   (optional)
sharp knife
dragon and flame templates
   (see page 164)
tray lined with baking
   parchment
20cm/8in round cake drum
small paintbrush
ruler

TIPS
You will need to make the dragon
parts at least a day before they
are needed.

You can change the expression
of the dragon by altering the
position of the pupil.

1 Dust the work surface with a little icing sugar, then knead the blue modelling paste until it is soft and pliable. Roll out the kneaded modelling paste until it is 5mm/¼in thick, using marzipan spacers if you like, and cut out the dragon's head, ears, body and legs, using the templates. Indent the toes and mouth with the sharp knife, then smooth the edges of all the parts with your fingers. Repeat with the green modelling paste to make the tummy and wings, indenting the line details on both parts with the sharp knife and smoothing the edges with your fingers. Without assembling the dragon, transfer the parts to the prepared tray and leave to dry overnight, uncovered, in a cool, dry place. Roll the trimmings into balls and store in an airtight container so the modelling paste does not dry out.

2 When the dragon parts have dried, following the instructions on page 150 and using the cake drum as a firm base, layer the sponge cakes, then fill with buttercream and jam to make one tall 20cm/8in cake. Following the instructions on page 152, cover the cake with the remaining buttercream. Chill in the fridge for 2 hours. When the buttercream has set, dust the work surface with a little icing sugar, then knead the white sugar paste until it is soft and pliable. Following the instructions on page 153, cover the cake with the kneaded sugar paste. Roll the trimmings into a ball and store in an airtight container so the sugar paste does not dry out and crack.

3 Dust the work surface with icing sugar, then knead half of the red sugar paste until it is soft and pliable. Roll out the kneaded sugar paste quite thinly and cut out about 10 flames, using the template. Brush the back of each flame with edible glue, then press them vertically onto the side of the cake (see picture). Repeat with the remaining red sugar paste until the side of the cake is covered in flames.

4 Brush the back of the dragon's body and head with a little edible glue, then attach them to the top of the cake. Using the picture as a guide, attach the ears, tummy, legs and wings, securing each part with edible glue. To make the nose, roll a tiny ball of blue modelling paste, then flatten it slightly and indent with the end of the paintbrush. To make the eye, roll out a very small ball of the remaining white sugar paste. For the pupil, roll out a tiny ball of black sugar paste and attach it to the eye, then attach an even tinier ball of white sugar paste to the top of the pupil, flattening it slightly as you do so. Attach the nose and eye to the head with edible glue. To make the tail, roll the remaining blue modelling paste into a long, tapered sausage about 15cm/6in long. Flatten the wider end of the sausage to form the base of the tail, then attach the base to the top of the cake with edible glue, making sure it lines up squarely with the body. Mould a tiny ball of green modelling paste into a triangle and attach it to the tail tip with edible glue. Curl the end of the tail slightly to form an s-shape over the top and side of the cake, securing it in place with edible glue. Roll the remaining green modelling paste into tiny balls, then attach them to the body and head of the dragon with edible glue, flattening them slightly as you do so. Leave the cake overnight to allow the sugar and modelling pastes to dry.

Marble Cake

VANILLA SPONGE
salted butter
caster sugar
vanilla extract
egg(s)
self-raising flour

CHOCOLATE SPONGE
salted butter
muscovado sugar
egg(s)
cocoa powder
self-raising flour

YOU WILL NEED
electric mixer
cake tin(s) lined with baking
parchment (for tips on lining
cake tins, see page 149)

TIP
If the cake is going to be split into layers, wrap it in baking parchment and foil, then leave it to rest overnight to firm up a little – this will make it easier to cut. (For tips on layering, filling and covering cakes, see pages 150 and 152–3.)

The table opposite shows you the quantity of ingredients and baking times required for different cake sizes and styles. It also offers advice on serving portions. Simply select your size and style and follow the method below.

1 Preheat the oven to 180°C/350°F/Gas 4 and allow the butter for the vanilla and chocolate sponges to soften slightly. For the vanilla sponge, put the softened butter, sugar and vanilla extract in a mixing bowl and beat with the electric mixer until light and fluffy. Lightly beat the egg(s), then gradually add to the mixture. If the mixture starts to curdle, add a little bit of the flour. Sift the flour into the bowl, then beat until just combined.

2 For the chocolate sponge, put the softened butter and muscovado sugar in a clean mixing bowl and beat with the electric mixer until light and fluffy. Lightly beat the egg(s), and gradually add to the mixture. If the mixture starts to curdle, add a little bit of the flour. Sift the cocoa powder and flour into the bowl, then beat until just combined.

3 Using 2 large spoons, drop alternate spoonfuls of the vanilla and chocolate cake mixtures into the prepared tin(s) until both mixtures have been used. Cut through the mixture with a knife several times to create a marbled effect. If necessary, level the surface with the back of a spoon, taking care not to spoil the marbled effect. Bake for the recommended time or until the top springs back slightly when gently pressed with a finger and a skewer inserted into the centre comes out clean. As oven temperatures can vary, check on the cake(s) about 5 minutes before the end of the recommended baking time.

4 Remove the cake(s) from the oven and leave to cool for 10 minutes, then remove from the tin, transfer to a wire rack and leave to cool completely.

Use this marble cake recipe for the following recipes throughout this book:

Valentine Cigarillo Cake
page 48

Festive Ball Cakes
page 92

Christmas Pudding Cake
page 97

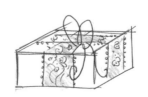

Gift-Wrapped Cake
page 135

Daisy Chain Mouse Cake
page 136

	10cm/4in round or square cake 6 cupcakes	13cm/5in round or square cake	15cm/6in round or square cake 4 x 8cm/3¼in mini ball cake halves 24 mini cupcakes	18cm/7in round or square cake	20cm/8in round, square or heart cake 12 cupcakes	23cm/9in round or square cake 2 x 15cm/6in ball cake halves
VANILLA SPONGE:						
salted butter	25g/1oz	25g/1oz	50g/1¾oz	75g/2½oz	100g/3½oz	150g/5½oz
caster sugar	25g/1oz/1 tbsp plus 2 tsp	25g/1oz/1 tbsp plus 2 tsp	50g/1¾oz/scant ¼ cup	75g/2½oz/scant ⅓ cup	100g/3½oz/scant ½ cup	150g/5½oz/heaped ⅔ cup
vanilla extract	½ tsp	½ tsp	1 tsp	1½ tsp	2 tsp	1 tbsp
eggs	1 small	1 small	1 large	1 large	2 large	3 large
self-raising flour	25g/1oz/scant ¼ cup	25g/1oz/scant ¼ cup	50g/1¾oz/scant ½ cup	75g/2½oz/heaped ½ cup	100g/3½oz/ heaped ¾ cup	150g/5½oz/scant 1¼ cups
CHOCOLATE SPONGE:						
salted butter	25g/1oz	25g/1oz	50g/ 1¾oz	75g/2½oz	100g/3½oz	150g/5½oz
muscovado sugar	25g/1oz/1 tbsp plus 2 tsp	25g/1oz/1 tbsp plus 2 tsp	50g/1¾oz/ heaped ¼ cup	75g/2½oz/ heaped ⅓ cup	100g/3½oz/ heaped ½ cup	150g/5½oz/ heaped ¾ cup
eggs	1 small	1 small	1 large	1 large	2 large	3 large
cocoa powder	2 tsp	2 tsp	20g/¾oz/scant ¼ cup	30g/1oz/¼ cup	40g/1½oz/⅓ cup	60g/2¼oz/½ cup
self-raising flour	1 tbsp	1 tbsp	30g/1oz/¼ cup	45g/1½oz/heaped ⅓ cup	60g/2¼oz/½ cup	90g/3¼oz/¾ cup
baking time	20 mins for large cakes	25 mins	30 mins for large cakes	40 mins for large cakes	45 mins for large cakes	50 mins
	15 mins for cupcakes		15 mins for mini ball cake halves		15 mins for cupcakes	45 mins for ball cake halves
			8 mins for mini cupcakes			
serves	large cakes: 10	12	large cakes: 15–20	20–30	large cakes: 30–40	large cakes: 40–50
	cupcakes: 6		mini ball cake halves: 4			ball cake halves: 12–16
			mini cupcakes: 24		cupcakes: 12	

Gingerbread House

MAKES 1 HOUSE
1 recipe quantity Gingerbread Dough (see page 27)
icing sugar, for dusting
100g/3½oz caramel-coloured sugar paste (see pages 160–1)
60g/2¼oz red-coloured sugar paste (see pages 160–1)
825g/1lb 13oz white sugar paste (see pages 160–1)
100g/3½oz white soft-peak Royal Icing (see page 46)
100g/3½oz white stiff-peak Royal Icing (see page 46)

YOU WILL NEED
rolling pin
gingerbread house templates (see page 166)
sharp knife
scallop-edge cutter (optional)
2 baking sheets lined with baking parchment
ruler
2 piping bags, 1 fitted with a no. 2 plain nozzle
23cm/9in square cake drum
1m/39in white ribbon, 8mm/³⁄₈in wide
straight frill cutter (optional)

TIP
You will need to make the walls and roof panels of the gingerbread house, door, candy cane and heart decorations the day before they are needed.

1 Preheat the oven to 180°C/350°F/Gas 4. Roll out the gingerbread dough following the instructions on page 148. Place the templates for the walls and roof panels on the dough and cut around them with the sharp knife. You will need 2 side walls, 2 end walls and 2 roof panels. (For tips on cutting out biscuits, see page 148.)

2 Indent a tiled pattern onto the roof panels with the scallop-edge cutter. Alternatively, score the pattern with the sharp knife. If you would like your house to have a window, position the heart-shaped template on one of the end walls and cut around it – this will be the back of the house. Using a spatula, transfer the walls and roof panels to the prepared baking sheets, spacing the biscuits well apart. Cook for 14 minutes, then remove from the oven. The cooking time is slightly longer than usual because the biscuits need to be firm to give the house rigidity. Transfer the biscuits to a wire cooling rack and leave to cool completely, then store in an airtight container.

3 Dust the work surface with icing sugar, then knead 20g/¾oz of the caramel sugar paste and 50g/1¾oz each of the red and white sugar pastes until they are soft and pliable. For the door, roll out the caramel sugar paste quite thinly and cut out a door, using the template. Score a cross-hatched pattern onto the front of the door using the sharp knife. Leave to dry overnight, uncovered, in a cool, dry place.

4 Dust the work surface with a little more icing sugar. For the candy cane decorations, roll about 15g/½oz each of the kneaded red and white sugar pastes into 2 long thin sausages. Twist the colours together, then gently roll them on the work surface **(a)** to form one long candy cane strip. Twist the strip again to form a tight candy cane. Repeat with the remaining kneaded red and white sugar pastes. Take the candy canes and cut a length about 14cm/5½in and mould it around the door to form an arch; cut 4 corner poles, each about 4cm/1½in, and mould the remaining canes into 4 lollipop swirls. Roll out the remaining red sugar paste quite thinly and cut out 2 hearts, using the template. If your house has a window, you only need to cut out 1 heart. Leave all the decorations to dry overnight, uncovered, in a cool, dry place **(b)**.

(a)

(b)

(c)

5 When the door and decorations have dried, decorate the walls of the house. Spoon the soft-peak royal icing into the piping bag fitted with the no. 2 plain nozzle. Attach the door and candy cane arch to the bottom of a (plain) end wall panel with a little royal icing – this will be the front of the house. Attach one of the red hearts about 2.5cm/1in above the door, using royal icing. If your house does not have a window, attach the other red heart in the same position to the back end wall of the house. Attach 2 candy cane lollipop swirls to each of the side walls using royal icing.

6 When all the decorations are attached, pipe a large dot of soft-peak royal icing onto the door for a handle. Next, pipe the detail on the red hearts and a little fleur de lys above them (or above the window), then pipe curly lines onto the end and side walls. (For tips on piping, see pages 157–9). Leave the walls to one side and allow to dry thoroughly **(c)**. Do not try to assemble the house while the decorations are still wet.

7 When the decorations have dried, spoon the stiff-peak royal icing into the remaining piping bag, then snip off the tip if necessary. Working quickly, take the front end wall and pipe some royal icing onto the inside of the side edges, then place the side walls in position **(d)**. Repeat with the back end wall and place in position, then support the wall panels with drinking glasses or tins of food and leave to dry overnight in a cool, dry place **(e)**. Roll up the bag and store in an airtight container until needed.

8 Meanwhile, dust the work surface with a little more icing sugar, then knead 700g/1lb 9oz of the white sugar paste until it is soft and pliable. Following the instructions on page 154, cover the cake drum with sugar paste and line the edge with white ribbon. Leave to set overnight, uncovered, in a cool, dry place.

(d)

(e)

9 When the walls have dried, pipe some stiff-peak royal icing along the roof edges and place the roof panels in position **(f and g)**. Hold the roof panels in position **(h)**, then support the lower roof edges with drinking glasses or tins of food to stop the roof panels from slipping down. Leave to dry for a few hours, or ideally overnight. Roll up the piping bag and store in an airtight container.

10 When the house is stable and all the elements are secure, pipe a little stiff-peak royal icing onto the bottom edge of each wall panel and carefully place the house onto the centre of the covered cake drum. Attach the candy cane poles to the corners of the house with a little more royal icing **(i)**. For the gable ends, roll out the remaining caramel sugar paste quite thinly and stamp out 4 decorative borders, each one about 14 x 2cm/ 5½ x ¾in, using the straight frill cutter. Alternatively, cut out a decorative border design by hand with the sharp knife. Pipe some royal icing onto the edges of the roof and attach the borders along each gable **(j)**, trimming as necessary.

11 For the roof snow, roll out the remaining white sugar paste quite thinly and cut out a 16 x 9cm/ 6¼ x 3½in rectangle, then re-roll the trimmings and cut out 2 more rectangles, each about 16 x 5cm/ 6¼ x 2in. Cut curvy edges down the sides of each rectangle. Attach the large piece of snow over the ridge of the roof **(k)**, and the smaller pieces to the bottom edges with royal icing. Leave to dry.

(f)   **(g)**   **(h)**

(i)   **(j)**   **(k)**

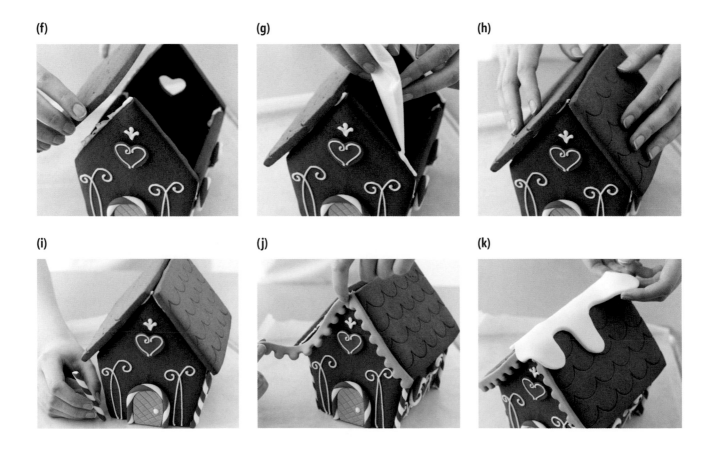

Thanksgiving Biscuits

MAKES 12 BISCUITS
icing sugar, for dusting
225g/8oz pale green-coloured
  sugar paste (see pages 160–1)
12 biscuits made using ½ recipe
  quantity Biscuit Dough of your
  choice (see pages 26–7), cut
  out with the circle template
  (see page 167) or a 6cm/2½in
  circle cutter
edible glue or 25g/1oz apricot
  jam, warmed
225g/8oz ivory-coloured sugar
  paste (see pages 160–1)
50g/1¾oz ivory-coloured soft-
  peak Royal Icing (see page 46)
50g/1¾oz light green-coloured
  soft-peak Royal Icing (see
  page 46)

YOU WILL NEED
small rolling pin
5.5cm/2¼in or 6cm/2½in circle
  cutter
small paintbrushes
small offset palette knife
Thanksgiving leaf designs
  (see page 167)
A4 sheet of paper
pins
scriber or sharp needle
2 piping bags, each fitted with
  a no. 2 plain nozzle

TIPS
Scribing is a little bit like creating a "join the dots" puzzle. It's really worth taking time and care over as the indentations made by the scriber will act as your piping guide. Detailed scribing will result in a delicate finish. Always allow the sugar paste to harden slightly before scribing.

The textured effect created by piping and dragging the icing over the biscuit is called "brush embroidery". You can use this technique on any biscuit or cake that's covered in sugar paste.

1 Dust the work surface with a little icing sugar, then knead the pale green sugar paste until it is soft and pliable. Roll out the kneaded sugar paste quite thinly and stamp out 6 circles with the 5.5cm/2¼in circle cutter. Brush the surface of half of the biscuits with edible glue. Using the offset palette knife, place the sugar paste circles over the prepared biscuits, taking care not to stretch or pull the sugar paste, then lightly smooth down each circle with your fingers. Repeat with the ivory sugar paste, remaining biscuits and edible glue to make 12 sugar paste-coated biscuits in total. Leave the sugar paste coating to harden slightly for at least 2 hours, uncovered, in a cool, dry place.

2 Meanwhile, trace each of the leaf designs onto the sheet of paper. Closely cut around the outline of each one to make four scribing guides. When the sugar paste coating has hardened slightly, place a scribing guide over the top of one of the biscuits. Secure the guide in place with a couple of pins, pushing them through the top and bottom points of the leaf design – if the guide moves during scribing, the leaf design will be messy and hard to pipe over. Support the edge of the biscuit with one hand, then lightly prick the outline and vein details of the leaf design onto the biscuit with the scriber **(a)**. Repeat with the remaining biscuits, using each of the scribing guides three times.

3 To decorate the pale green biscuits, spoon the ivory soft-peak royal icing into one of the piping bags and dampen a paintbrush with a little water. Using the indentations made by the scriber as a guide, pipe a line of royal icing over one-quarter of the leaf outline, then lightly drag the icing towards the centre of the biscuit with the dampened paintbrush to create a textured effect **(b)**. (For tips on piping, see pages 157–9.) Working in sections, continue to pipe and drag the icing towards the centre of the biscuit until you have completed the outline of the leaf. Carefully pipe the vein details over the top, using the indentations made by the scriber as a guide. Decorating one biscuit at a time and dampening the paintbrush as necessary, repeat with the remaining ivory soft-peak royal icing and pale green biscuits. Repeat step 3 with the light green soft peak royal icing and ivory biscuits to make 12 iced biscuits in total. Leave the biscuits overnight, uncovered, in a cool, dry place to allow the icing to set.

(a)

(b)

White Blossom Christening Cake

MAKES 1 CAKE
18cm/7in round Basic Sponge
   Cake (see pages 62–3)
13cm/5in round Citrus Sponge
   Cake (see pages 62–3)
1 recipe quantity Vanilla
   Buttercream (see page 16)
icing sugar, for dusting
1kg/2lb 4oz pale blue-coloured
   sugar paste (see pages 160–1)
100g/3½oz white sugar paste
   (see pages 160–1)
100g/3½oz white soft-peak
   Royal Icing (see page 46)

YOU WILL NEED
18cm/7in cake drum
13cm/5in round cake drum
small rolling pin
1.2cm/½in and 2.3cm/1in
   blossom plunger cutters
indented foam pad or a piece
   of crinkled kitchen foil
double-ended ball tool
   (optional)
plastic dowels
2 piping bags, 1 fitted
   with a no. 2 plain nozzle

1 Following the instructions on page 150 and using the cake drums as firm bases, layer the sponge cakes, then fill with buttercream. Following the instructions on page 152, cover the cakes with the remaining buttercream. Chill in the fridge for 2 hours. When the buttercream has set, dust the work surface with a little icing sugar, then knead 700g/1lb 9oz of the pale blue sugar paste until it is soft and pliable. Following the instructions on page 153, cover the 18cm/7in cake with the kneaded sugar paste. Repeat with the remaining sugar paste to cover the 13cm/5in cake. Roll the sugar paste trimmings into a ball and store in an airtight container until needed.

2 Dust the work surface with a little more icing sugar, then knead the white sugar paste until it is soft and pliable. Roll out the kneaded sugar paste quite thinly and stamp out 30–40 blossoms using the 1.2cm/½in blossom plunger cutter **(a)**. Place the blossoms on the indented foam pad, then indent the centre of each one with the small head of the ball tool or with the tip of your little finger **(b)**. Roll the trimmings into a ball and repeat with the 2.3cm/1in blossom plunger cutter to make 25–30 blossoms, indenting the centre of each one with the large head of the ball tool or with your little finger. Leave the cakes and the blossoms overnight, uncovered, in a cool, dry place to allow the sugar paste and blossoms to dry.

3 When the sugar paste and blossoms have dried, follow the instructions on page 156 and stack the 13cm/5in cake on top of the 18cm/7in cake with plastic dowels. For a clean join between the tiers, put a little pale blue sugar paste in a small bowl. Add water, a few drops at a time, and mix until a thick paste forms. Spoon the paste into the nozzle-free piping bag and snip off the tip if necessary. Pipe the paste around the base of the top tier, then run your finger along the join to remove any excess paste. (For tips on piping, see pages 157–9.) Spoon the royal icing into the piping bag fitted with the no. 2 plain nozzle. Pipe 6 dots in the centre of the large blossoms **(c)** to form a blossom shape (see picture) and a single dot in the centre of the small blossoms. Attach the blossoms over the top and sides of the cake, securing each one with a dot of royal icing. Leave to set, uncovered, in a cool, dry place, before serving.

(a)

(b)

(c)

Party Penguins

MAKES 6 PENGUINS
10g/¼oz salted butter
100g/3½oz marshmallows
(pink, white or mixed)
¼ tsp vanilla extract
85g/3oz crisped rice cereal
icing sugar, for dusting
200g/7oz black-coloured sugar
paste (see pages 160–1)
60g/2¼oz orange-coloured
sugar paste (see pages 160–1)
edible glue or cooled, boiled
water
50g/1¾oz white sugar paste
(see pages 160–1)
10g/¼oz each of red-, pink-,
pale pink- and green-coloured
sugar pastes (see pages
160–1)
5g/⅛oz yellow-coloured sugar
paste (see pages 160–1)

YOU WILL NEED
small rolling pin
sharp knife
2.5cm/1in, 3.5cm/1⅓in and
7mm/¼in circle cutters
small paintbrush
ruler
straight frill cutter (optional)

TIP
For quick, easy and delicious treats, press the marshmallow mixture into an even layer in a shallow tin lined with baking parchment. Leave to cool for about 30 minutes and then cut out shapes with cookie cutters.

1 In a large heavy-based saucepan, melt the butter over a low heat, then add the marshmallows and stir frequently until melted. Remove from the heat. Add the vanilla extract and the crisped rice cereal and stir until combined. Leave to cool slightly for 10 minutes.

2 To make a body, take 15g/½oz of the marshmallow mixture and mould it into a teardrop shape – you can be quite firm when handling the mixture. Press the shape to form as smooth a surface as possible **(a)**, as any large bumps will be visible under the sugar paste covering. Mould the bottom of the shape into a flat base. Repeat with the remaining marshmallow mixture to make 6 bodies.

3 Dust the work surface with a little icing sugar, then knead about 50g/1¾oz of the black sugar paste until it is soft and pliable. Roll out the sugar paste quite thinly and use it to cover one of the marshmallow bodies, smoothing down the sides with your hands. Trim off any excess sugar paste at the base of the body **(b)**. Repeat with the remaining sugar paste, re-rolling the trimmings as necessary, until all of the bodies are covered. Roll the trimmings into a ball and store in an airtight container.

4 For the feet, roll out the orange sugar paste quite thinly and cut out 12 circles with the 2.5cm/1in circle cutter. For toes, indent two small lines on the end of each foot with the end of the paintbrush **(c)**. Place two of the feet side by side and flatten the back half with your thumb to make a flat base for the body to rest on. To attach, brush the flattened sides of the feet with a little edible glue and carefully place a penguin body on top **(d)**. Repeat until all the feet are attached. Roll the trimmings into a ball and store in an airtight container so the sugar paste does not dry out and crack.

5 For the flippers, re-roll the remaining black sugar paste and cut out 6 circles using the 2.5cm/1in circle cutter. Cut each one in half to make 12 semi-circles and attach 2 semi-circles, cut-side forward, to each penguin with edible glue **(e)**. You can vary the penguins by changing the position of their flippers. For attached flippers, cover the underside of each flipper with edible glue before attaching. For hanging flippers, cover only the top half of each flipper in edible glue. Roll the trimmings into a ball and store in an airtight container so the sugar paste does not dry out and crack.

(a)

(b)

6 For the white tummies, roll out the white sugar paste quite thinly and cut out 6 circles using the 3.5cm/1⅓in circle cutter. Brush a little edible glue over one of the tummies and attach it to a penguin, positioning it slightly nearer the feet to leave space for the penguin's face **(f)**. Repeat until all the tummies are attached. Roll the trimmings into a ball and store in an airtight container so the sugar paste does not dry out and crack.

7 Divide the remaining orange sugar paste into 6 large pea-sized balls and shape each one into a cone for the beaks. Attach each beak in place with a little edible glue **(g)**.

8 For the eyes, roll 12 very small balls out of the remaining white sugar paste. Put a little edible glue on the back of each one and push the eyes gently into position just above the beak, flattening them slightly as you do so. For pupils, roll out 12 tiny balls from the remaining black sugar paste and attach each one in place with a little edible glue. You can change the expression of each penguin by altering the position of the pupils **(h)**.

(c)   **(d)**   **(e)**

(f)   **(g)**   **(h)**

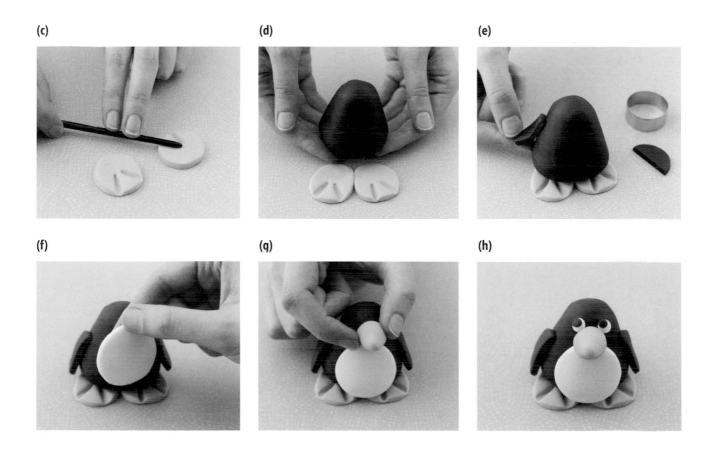

9 Make a selection of hats and fancy dress items using the red, pink, pale pink, green and yellow sugar pastes and any leftover scraps of sugar paste trimmings. Knead all the sugar pastes until they are soft and pliable and roll out each one quite thinly.

For a hat, cut out a 10 x 1.5cm/4 x ⅝in rectangle of sugar paste in any colour. Cut a decorative border along one long edge using the straight frill cutter or the sharp knife. Wrap the sugar paste around the penguin's head to form a hat, concealing the join at the back, and secure with a little edible glue.

For a superhero mask, cut out a 10 x 1.5cm/4 x ⅝in rectangle of sugar paste in any colour. Trim the edge so that it is wider in the middle section and tapers off at both ends (see picture). Cut out 2 eye holes using the 7mm/¼in circle cutter. Position the mask over the penguin's face and secure in place with a little edible glue.

For a clown's nose, push a large, pea-sized ball of red sugar paste onto the penguin's beak and secure in place with a little edible glue if necessary.

For a sheriff's badge, cut out a small, yellow sugar paste star using the sharp knife and attach to the penguin's body with a little edible glue.

For the bunny headband, roll 2 large pea-sized balls of white sugar paste and mould each one into a flattened teardrop shape for the ears. For the centres, roll 2 small pea-sized balls of pale pink sugar paste and roll each one into a sausage. Flatten the centres and attach each one to the ears with a little edible glue. For the headband, take a little more white sugar paste and roll it out into a thin sausage about 6cm/2½in long. Flatten the headband and attach it to the top of the penguin's head, trimming as necessary, then place the ears in position, securing both with a little edible glue.

10 Leave the penguins overnight, uncovered, in a cool, dry place to allow the sugar paste to dry.

Mini Ghost Cakes

MAKES 6 CAKES
**6 Rich Chocolate Cupcakes
  (see page 129), paper cupcake
  cases removed**
**¼ recipe quantity Vanilla
  Buttercream (see page 16)**
**1 recipe quantity Vanilla Sugar
  Syrup (see page 119)**
6 tsp seedless raspberry jam
icing sugar, for dusting
**1kg/2lb 4oz white sugar paste
  (see pages 160–1)**
**edible glue or cooled, boiled
  water**
**25g/1oz black-coloured sugar
  paste (see pages 160–1)**

YOU WILL NEED
small serrated knife
6 x 7.5cm/3in round cake cards
pastry brush
small offset palette knife
small rolling pin
12.5cm/5in circle cutter
**5mm/¼in marzipan spacers
  (optional)**
small paintbrush

TIP
You can change the expressions of
the ghosts by altering the position
of the pupils and changing the
shape of the mouths.

1 Using the serrated knife, carefully trim off the domed tops of each cupcake to create a flat stable base for the ghost cakes. Reserve the domed tops and leave to one side until needed. Turn the cupcakes upside down and attach a cake card to the base of each one with a little buttercream.

2 Lightly brush the top and side of each cupcake with a little sugar syrup. Using the offset palette knife, spread a thin layer of buttercream, followed by a layer of jam, over the top of each cupcake, then place the reserved domes on top, trimming as necessary to create a neat dome shape. Clean the offset palette knife, then use it to cover each cake with the remaining buttercream. Chill in the fridge for 2 hours until set.

3 Dust the work surface with a little icing sugar, then knead half of the white sugar paste until it is soft and pliable. Roll out the kneaded sugar paste quite thinly and stamp out 6 circles with the 12.5cm/5in circle cutter. Following the instructions on page 153, cover the cakes with sugar paste.

4 Dust the work surface with a little more icing sugar, then knead the remaining white sugar paste until it is soft and pliable. Roll out the kneaded sugar paste until it is 5mm/¼in thick, using marzipan spacers if you like, and stamp out 6 more circles with the 12.5cm/5in circle cutter. Roll over each circle with a small rolling pin to make the sugar paste slightly thinner. Brush the top of each cake with a little edible glue, then carefully lift a circle of sugar paste over the top of each one, pinching it into fabric-like folds at the base. Roll the trimmings into a ball and store in an airtight container so the sugar paste does not dry out and crack.

5 Knead the black sugar paste until it is soft and pliable. To make the eyes, roll 12 small balls of black sugar paste, then slightly flatten each one with your thumb. For the pupils, roll 12 tiny balls of white sugar paste and attach them to the eyes with a little edible glue, flattening them slightly as you do so. To make the mouths, roll 6 pea-sized balls of black sugar paste into small sausages, then mould and flatten each one into a different shape, trimming the sugar paste with a small sharp knife if necessary. Attach the eyes and mouths to the ghost cakes with a little edible glue. Leave the cakes for at least 2 hours, uncovered, in a cool, dry place to allow the icing to set.

Festive Ball Cakes

MAKES 2 FESTIVE
BALL CAKES
butter, for greasing
sponge cake mixture of your
   choice for 4 x 8cm/3¼in mini
   ball cake halves (see pages
   56–7, 62–3 or 76–7)
1 recipe quantity Sugar Syrup
   (see page 119)
½ recipe quantity Vanilla
   Buttercream (see page 16)
icing sugar, for dusting
125g/4½oz red-coloured sugar
   paste (see pages 160–1)
125g/4½oz orange-coloured
   sugar paste (see pages 160–1)

YOU WILL NEED
6 x 8cm/3¼in-cup ball cake pan
long serrated knife
pastry brush
small offset palette knife
small rolling pin
5mm/¼in marzipan spacers
   (optional)
sharp knife
icing smoother

TIP
Try making these small ball
cakes out of chocolate sponge
sandwiched with orange citrus
buttercream (see pages 62–3
and 16).

1 Lightly grease 4 cups of the ball cake pan with butter, then pour the cake mixture into the cups until they are each about two-thirds full. Using the back of a metal spoon, form a dip in the centre of each cake, pushing the mixture out towards the edges – this prevents the cakes from rising too much in the centre.

2 Bake for 15 minutes or until a skewer inserted into the centre of each cake comes out clean. Remove from the oven and leave in the pan to cool completely.

3 Level the surface of any cakes that have risen above the top of the pan with the serrated knife, then turn the cakes out of the pan onto a work surface

4 Using the serrated knife, level the flat-side of 2 ball cake halves to ensure they will create a neat ball shape when sandwiched together. Lightly brush the cut-sides of the cakes with some of the sugar syrup, then spread a thin layer of buttercream over the syrup with the offset palette knife and sandwich the cakes together to form a ball shape. Using the offset palette knife, cover the cake with buttercream **(a)**, then chill in the fridge for 2 hours until set. Repeat with the remaining cake halves to make two buttercream covered ball cakes in total.

5 When the buttercream has set, dust the work surface with a little icing sugar, then knead the red sugar paste until it is soft and pliable. Roll out the kneaded sugar paste until it is 5mm/¼in thick, using marzipan spacers if you like. Lift the rolled sugar paste and gently place it over the top of one of the cake balls. Using your hands, smooth the sugar paste over the cake, covering it completely, but take care not to stretch or pull the sugar paste. Gather the sugar paste at the base of the cake **(b)**. Trim off the excess sugar paste with the sharp knife, then flatten the base slightly **(c)** – this will allow the cake to stand unsupported. Smooth the sugar paste again using the icing smoother. Decide which section of the cake will be the front, then concentrate on making that section look as smooth and neat as possible, hiding any creases in the sugar paste at the back of the cake. Repeat with the remaining ball cake, and the orange sugar paste. Decorate the ball cakes immediately.

(a)

(b)

(c)

MAKES 1 BAUBLE CAKE
½ length of dried spaghetti
icing sugar, for dusting
30g/1oz caramel-coloured sugar
** paste (see pages 160–1)**
edible glue or cooled, boiled
** water**
8cm/3¼in ball cake, covered in
** red-coloured sugar paste**
** (see page 92)**
gold edible lustre dust
30g/1oz red-coloured soft-peak
** Royal Icing (see page 46)**

YOU WILL NEED
baking parchment
small rolling pin
5mm/¼in marzipan spacers
** (optional)**
sharp knife
ruler
straight frill cutter (optional)
3.5cm/1⅓in circle cutter
** (optional)**
small paintbrushes
piping bag fitted with a no. 2
** plain nozzle**

CHRISTMAS DECORATIONS

For the Red Bauble Cake

1 This recipe makes one cake but if you want to make more than one, simply scale up the amount of the listed ingredients. To make the loop for the top of the bauble, soak the piece of spaghetti in a mug of boiling water for 10 minutes or until it is soft and pliable. Bend the spaghetti into a loop (see picture on page 95), then transfer it to a piece of baking parchment to dry.

2 Dust the work surface with a little icing sugar, then knead the caramel sugar paste until it is soft and pliable. Roll out the sugar paste until it is 5mm/¼in thick, using marzipan spacers if you like, then cut a 15 x 3cm/6 x 1¼in strip. Stamp a decorative border on the edge of the strip with the straight frill cutter or cut out a frill pattern with the sharp knife (see picture on page 95).

3 Roll the caramel sugar paste trimmings into a ball, then re-roll until it is 5mm/¼in thick. Cut out a circle using the circle cutter. Alternatively, cut out a circle about 3.5cm/1⅓in in diameter using the sharp knife. Turn the circle upside down, then brush the edges with a little edible glue. Attach the decorative border to the edge of the circle, creating a sun-like effect (see picture on page 95). Attach this to the top of the covered ball cake with a little more edible glue. Roll a pea sized ball of caramel sugar paste into a cylinder, then attach this to the centre of the circle with edible glue. Push the bottom of the spaghetti loop into the cylinder and secure in place with edible glue. Leave the cake to dry overnight, uncovered, in a cool, dry place.

4 When the sugar paste is completely dry, put a little gold edible lustre dust in a small bowl. Add water, a few drops at a time, and mix until a thick paint forms. Paint the caramel sugar paste and the spaghetti loop with the lustre paint and leave to dry completely.

5 When the lustre paint has dried, spoon the royal icing into the piping bag and pipe loops and curvy lines from the top of the bauble downwards (see picture on page 95). If you are not confident about piping loops and curves, pipe straight lines of various lengths down the side of the bauble. Embellish your design with dots of royal icing, if you like. (For tips on piping, see pages 157–9.) Leave the cake overnight, uncovered, in a cool, dry place to allow the icing to set.

**MAKES 1 ORANGE
POMANDER CAKE**
8cm/3¼in ball cake, covered in
    orange-coloured sugar paste
    (see page 92)
icing sugar, for dusting
50g/1¾oz red-coloured flower
    paste (see pages 160–1)
edible glue or cooled, boiled
    water
30g/1oz dark brown-coloured
    soft-peak Royal Icing (see
    page 46)

YOU WILL NEED
cocktail stick
small rolling pin
sharp knife
ruler
design wheeler tool with stitch
    head
small paintbrush
bow templates (see page 165)
tissue paper
piping bag fitted with a no. 1.5
    plain nozzle

For the Orange Pomander Cake

1 This recipe makes one cake but if you want to make more than one, simply scale up the amount of the listed ingredients. Blunt the end of the cocktail stick slightly, then indent tiny holes all over the orange sugar paste – this will take time, but care taken at this stage will produce a more realistic effect overall. Leave the cake to dry overnight, uncovered, in a cool, dry place.

2 Dust the work surface with a little icing sugar, then knead the red flower paste until it is smooth and elastic. Roll out the red flower paste very thinly, then cut into 4 strips, each about 12 x 1.5cm/ 4¾ x ⅝in. Use the design wheeler tool to indent a "stitched" line along the edges of each strip. Arrange the strips over the ball to form a cross at the top of the cake, then secure them to the cake with a little edible glue.

3 Roll the red flower paste trimmings into a ball, then re-roll quite thinly. Place the templates for the bow on top of the rolled flower paste and cut around them with the sharp knife, then use the design wheeler tool to indent a "stitched" line along the edges of each strip. Attach the tailpieces to the top of the cake, draping them down the side, then pinch them together slightly at the top. Secure the tailpieces in place with edible glue.

4 Take one of the loop pieces and brush one of the short ends with a little edible glue, then fold it in half to form a loop, pinching it in slightly at the join. Repeat with the remaining loop piece to make 2 loops. Stuff the hollow of each loop with a small piece of crumpled tissue paper – this will keep the flower paste in position while it dries. Place the loops at the top of the cake to form a bow, securing each one with edible glue. Mould the bow join over and around the spot where the bow loops meet, and secure with a little edible glue.

5 Spoon the royal icing into the piping bag. To achieve the studded-clove effect along the edges of the ribbon, pipe a little cross, then immediately pipe a dot over the top to make a "clove". Repeat along the edges of each ribbon, starting at the top edges and working your way down to the base. (For tips on piping, see pages 157–9.) Leave the cake overnight, uncovered, in a cool, dry place to allow the icing to set. Remove the tissue paper from the bow before serving.

Christmas Pudding Cake

MAKES 1 CAKE
2 x 15cm/6in ball cake halves
in your choice of sponge (see
pages 56–7, 62–3 and 76–7)
1 recipe quantity Sugar Syrup
(see page 119)
1 recipe quantity Vanilla
Buttercream (see page 16)
icing sugar, for dusting
1kg/2lb 4oz dark brown-
coloured sugar paste
(see pages 160–1)
150g/5½oz white sugar paste
(see pages 160–1)
edible glue or cooled, boiled
water
5g/⅛oz black-coloured sugar
paste (see pages 160–1)
15g/½oz red-coloured sugar
paste (see pages 160–1)
50g/1¾oz dark green-coloured
sugar paste (see pages 160–1)

YOU WILL NEED
long serrated knife
pastry brush
offset palette knife
rolling pin
5mm/¼in marzipan spacers
(optional)
sharp knife
icing smoother
paintbrush
holly leaf template (see page
162)

1 Using the serrated knife, level the flat-side of the ball cake halves to ensure they will create a neat ball shape when sandwiched together, then slice each cake in half horizontally to form four layers. Lightly brush the cut-sides of the cakes with sugar syrup. Stacking the layers back together, fill and cover the cake with buttercream using the offset palette knife. (For tips on filling and covering ball cakes with buttercream, see page 92.) Chill in the fridge for 2 hours until set.

2 When the buttercream has set, dust the work surface with a little icing sugar, then knead the dark brown sugar paste until it is soft and pliable. Roll out the kneaded sugar paste until it is 5mm/¼in thick, using marzipan spacers if you like. Lift the rolled sugar paste and gently place it over the top of the cake. Using your hands, smooth the sugar paste over the cake, covering it completely, but take care not to stretch or pull the sugar paste. Gather the sugar paste at the base of the cake. Trim off the excess sugar paste with the sharp knife, then flatten the base slightly – this will allow the cake to stand unsupported. Smooth the sugar paste again using the icing smoother. (For tips on covering ball cakes in sugar paste, see page 92.) Roll the trimmings into a ball and store in an airtight container so the sugar paste does not dry out and crack.

3 For the brandy sauce, dust the work surface with a little more icing sugar, then knead the white sugar paste until it is soft and pliable. Roll out the kneaded sugar paste into a circle about 10cm/4in in diameter and about 5mm/¼in thick, using marzipan spacers if you like. Cut a wavy line around the edge using the sharp knife. Lightly brush the top of the cake with edible glue and place the wavy white sugar paste over the top, pressing down gently to secure. Roll the trimmings into a ball and store in an airtight container so the sugar paste does not dry out and crack.

4 For the nuts, roll the black sugar paste into 15 tiny balls. For the peel, knead a tiny amount of dark brown sugar paste into 5g/⅛oz of the remaining white sugar paste to form a small amount of light brown sugar paste, then roll this into 6 tiny balls. For the dried fruit, roll 5g/⅛oz of the red sugar paste into 9 tiny balls. Brush the nuts, peel and dried fruits with a little edible glue, then attach them around the side of the cake.

5 For the holly leaves, dust the work surface with a little more icing sugar, then knead the dark green sugar paste until it is soft and pliable. Roll out the kneaded sugar paste quite thinly, then cut out 3 holly leaves using the template and indent veins onto each one with the sharp knife. Brush the back of the leaves with a little edible glue and attach them to the top of the cake, curling them slightly if you like. For the holly berries, roll the remaining red sugar paste into 3 small balls. Brush the base of the berries with a little edible glue and attach them to the centre of the leaves. Leave the cake overnight, uncovered, in a cool, dry place to allow the sugar paste to dry.

Easter Hen Biscuits

**MAKES 6 HEN
AND 12 EGG BISCUITS**
200g/7oz dark brown-coloured
soft-peak Royal Icing (see
page 46)
6 hen biscuits and 12 egg
biscuits made using ½ recipe
quantity Biscuit Dough of
your choice (see pages 26–7),
cut out with the hen and egg
templates (see page 169)
50g/1¾oz red-coloured soft-
peak Royal Icing (see page 46)
100g/3½oz cream-coloured soft-
peak Royal Icing (see page 46)
10g/¼oz white soft-peak Royal
Icing (see page 46)
10g/¼oz black-coloured soft-
peak Royal Icing (see page 46)

YOU WILL NEED
5 piping bags, 3 fitted with
a no. 2 plain nozzle
3 squeeze icing bottles

1 Spoon 50g/1¾oz of the dark brown soft-peak royal icing into one of the piping bags fitted with a no. 2 plain nozzle. Pipe a hen outline onto each of the hen biscuits, avoiding the comb and wattle. (For tips on piping, see pages 157–9.) Roll up the piping bag and store in an airtight container until needed. Spoon half of the red soft-peak royal icing into another piping bag fitted with a no. 2 plain nozzle and pipe outlines of the comb and wattle onto the hen biscuits. Spoon 30g/1oz of the cream soft-peak royal icing into the remaining piping bag fitted with a no. 2 plain nozzle and pipe a beak outline onto the hen biscuits **(a)** and an egg outline onto the egg biscuits. Leave the biscuits for at least 10–15 minutes, uncovered, in a cool, dry place to allow the icing to set.

2 Meanwhile, spoon the remaining dark brown, red and cream soft-peak royal icings into three separate bowls, then add enough water to each bowl to slacken the icings to flood consistency (see page 46). Pour the dark brown, red and cream flood icings into separate icing bottles.

3 Decorating one biscuit at a time, quickly and carefully flood the centre of each hen biscuit with the dark brown flood icing **(b)**, then gently squeeze small drops of cream flood icing onto the body of the hen to create a speckled effect **(c)** – if you do not do this immediately, the speckles will dry proud of the hen's body. Repeat with the remaining dark brown and cream flood icings and the remaining hen biscuits until all the hens have speckled bodies. Flood the comb and wattle of the hen biscuits with red flood icing, then flood the beaks with cream flood icing. Flood the centre of the egg biscuits with the remaining cream flood icing. Leave for at least 1 hour, uncovered, in a cool, dry place to allow the icing to set.

4 When the icing has set, use the remaining dark brown soft-peak royal icing to pipe another hen outline around the edge of each biscuit, then pipe the wing detail over the top of the hen's body. Spoon the white royal icing into one of the remaining piping bags, then snip off the tip if necessary. Pipe an eye onto the face of each hen and leave to dry for 10–15 minutes. When the icing has dried, spoon the black royal icing into the remaining piping bag, then snip off the tip if necessary. Pipe a tiny pupil on top of each eye. Leave overnight, uncovered, in a cool, dry place to allow the icing to set.

(a)

(b)

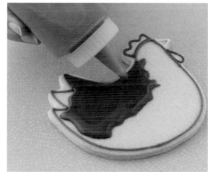

(c)

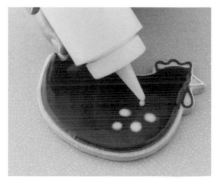

Mother's Day Biscuits

MAKES 4 BISCUITS
icing sugar, for dusting
50g/1¾oz pink-coloured sugar
    paste (see pages 160–1)
edible glue or 25g/1oz apricot
    jam, warmed
4 biscuits made using ¼ recipe
    quantity Biscuit Dough of your
    choice (see pages 26–7), cut
    out with the handbag, purse
    and shoe templates (see page
    168)
20g/¾oz cream-coloured sugar
    paste (see pages 160–1)
20g/¾oz black-coloured sugar
    paste (see pages 160–1)
80g/2¾oz purple-coloured
    sugar paste (see pages 160–1)
silver edible lustre dust

YOU WILL NEED
small rolling pin
handbag, purse and shoe
    templates (see page 168)
sharp knife
ruler
small paintbrushes
small offset palette knife
design wheeler tool with stitch
    head
double-ended ball tool
straight frill cutter (optional)
foam pad or clean, dry folded
    kitchen towel

For the Pink Handbag

1 Dust the work surface with a little icing sugar, then knead the pink sugar paste until it is soft and pliable. Roll out the kneaded sugar paste quite thinly and cut out a handbag, using the template. Using the ruler to help you, cut away the top of the handbag and trim the sides to form a rectangle. The width of the rectangle should be slightly smaller than the width of the biscuit. Roll the trimmings into a ball and store in an airtight container so the sugar paste does not dry out and crack.

2 Brush the underside of the pink rectangle with a little edible glue, then place it over the handbag biscuit using the offset palette knife, taking care not to stretch it. To achieve the "quilted" effect, use the design wheeler tool to indent "stitched" diagonal lines across the sugar paste **(a)**.

3 For the cream panel, roll out the cream sugar paste quite thinly and cut a 10 x 1cm/4 x ½in panel. Make 2 indentations on either end of the panel with the large head of the ball tool **(a)**. Attach the panel to the biscuit with edible glue so that it is flush with the pink sugar paste. Trim as necessary.

4 For the handle, roll a large pea-sized ball of black sugar paste. Split the ball in half and roll each one into a thin sausage about 15cm/6in long. Twist the two together, then gently roll them on the work surface **(b)** to form one long handle cord. Trim the ends to neaten. Using the indentations made by the ball tool as a guide, attach the handle to the panel and to the biscuit with edible glue.

5 For the tassels, roll 2 tiny balls of black sugar paste and 2 even smaller balls of cream sugar paste. Flatten all of the balls slightly. Using a little edible glue, attach the cream balls to the black balls and leave to one side. Roll 2 small balls of black sugar paste and mould them into teardrop shapes. Flatten them slightly, then make 3 or 4 cuts for the tassels, using the sharp knife **(c)**. Using edible glue, attach the tassels to the ends of the handle, then attach the black and cream balls to the top of the tassels (see picture on page 103).

(a)

(b)

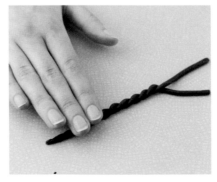

(c)

(d)

For the Pink Stiletto Shoe

1 Dust the work surface with a little icing sugar and roll out the remaining pink, black and cream sugar pastes quite thinly. Using the template, cut out one shoe in each colour.

2 Cut out the central section of the pink shoe; the toe and heel of the cream shoe; and the stiletto heel, sole and toe detail of the black shoe. For the heel tip, score a line in the black sugar paste at the base of the stiletto heel with the sharp knife. Roll the trimmings into balls and store in an airtight container so the sugar paste does not dry out and crack.

3 To achieve the "quilted" effect on the central section, use the design wheeler tool to indent "stitched" diagonal lines across the pink sugar paste. Using the offset palette knife, arrange the various sugar paste sections **(d)** over the stiletto biscuit, trimming as necessary to achieve a neat finish. Brush the surface of the biscuit with edible glue, then secure each sugar paste section in place, taking care not to stretch or pull them.

For the Purple Purse

1 Dust the work surface with icing sugar, then knead 25g/1oz of the purple sugar paste until it is soft and pliable. For the frills, roll out the kneaded paste quite thinly, then cut into 4 strips, each about 10 x 2cm/4 x ¾in. Stamp out a frill on the edge of the strips with the straight frill cutter **(e)** or cut out a frill pattern with the sharp knife. Place the strips on the foam pad, then gently roll the large head of the ball tool over the frill to soften the edges **(f)**.

2 Using edible glue to secure all the layers, attach one frill to the bottom of the purse biscuit, then overlap the remaining frills until you have covered the entire biscuit **(g)**. Do not cover the clasp in purple sugar paste. Trim the frills as necessary.

(e)

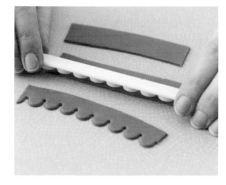

(f)

(g)

3 For the clasp, roll a pea-sized amount of the cream sugar paste into a little sausage and attach it at the top of the biscuit with edible glue, trimming the edges as necessary. Roll 2 tiny balls of cream sugar paste and attach them to the centre of the sausage to form a clasp. When the sugar paste is completely dry, put a little silver edible lustre dust in a small bowl. Add water, a few drops at a time, and mix until a thick paint forms. Paint the clasp with the lustre paint and leave to dry completely. Cover the paint with cling film and set aside until needed.

For the Purple Court Shoe

1 Dust the work surface with icing sugar, then knead the remaining purple sugar paste until it is soft and pliable. Roll out the kneaded paste quite thinly and cut out a court shoe, using the template. Cut away a little sugar paste at the top of the shoe to create a foot hole **(h)**. Using the sugar paste shoe as a guide, brush the court shoe biscuit with edible glue. Using the offset palette knife, place the sugar paste shoe over the biscuit, taking care not to stretch or pull it **(i)**, then gently smooth it over the biscuit with your fingers.

2 Use the design wheeler tool to indent "stitched" seams onto the shoe, then score a line for the heel tip at the bottom of the heel using the back of the sharp knife.

3 To make the rose, re-roll the purple sugar paste trimmings quite thinly and cut a 10 x 1cm/ 4 x ½in strip. Stamp a frill onto the edge of the strip with the straight frill cutter or cut out a frill pattern with the sharp knife. Gently roll up the strip to form a rose **(j)**. Pinch the sugar paste together at the bottom of the rose, then cut off the excess sugar paste to form a flat base and attach the rose to the shoe with a little edible glue. Roll a tiny ball of cream sugar paste and attach it to the centre of the rose with a little edible glue. When the sugar paste is completely dry, paint the centre of the rose with the lustre paint and leave to dry completely.

(h)

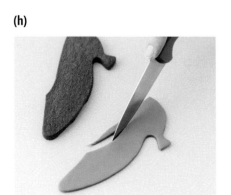

(i)

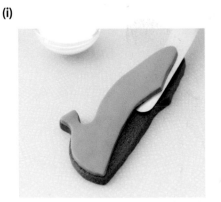

(j)

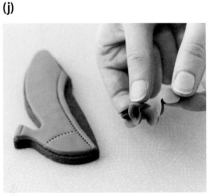

Birthday Butterfly Mini Domes

MAKES 4 CAKES
icing sugar, for dusting
200g/7oz pale yellow-coloured sugar paste (see pages 160–1)
200g/7oz pale blue-coloured sugar paste (see pages 160–1)
4 prepared Sponge or Marble Dome Mini Cakes (see page 128)
50g/1¾oz yellow-coloured modelling paste (see pages 160–1)
50g/1¾oz dark blue-coloured modelling paste (see pages 160–1)
30g/1oz black-coloured stiff-peak Royal Icing (see page 46)

YOU WILL NEED
small rolling pin
5mm/¼in marzipan spacers (optional)
sharp knife
ruler
butterfly templates (see page 169)
baking tray lined with baking parchment, plus extra baking parchment for lining the "troughs"
piping bag fitted with a no. 2 plain nozzle
A4 sheet of stiff card

TIPS
For tips on baking ball cake halves, see page 92.

You will need to cover the cakes, and make the butterfly wings at least a day before they are needed. (For more tips on assembling sugarcraft butterflies, see page 116.)

1 Dust the work surface with a little icing sugar, then knead the pale yellow sugar paste until it is soft and pliable. Roll out the kneaded sugar paste until it is 5mm/¼in thick, using marzipan spacers if you like. Cut out 2 squares, each measuring 13 x 13cm/5 x 5in. Repeat with the pale blue sugar paste to make four squares of sugar paste in total. Following the instructions on page 153, use one square of sugar paste to cover each cake, trimming as necessary. Leave the cakes overnight, uncovered, in a cool, dry place to allow the sugar paste to dry.

2 To make the butterflies, dust the work surface with a little more icing sugar, then knead the yellow modelling paste until it is soft and pliable. Roll out the kneaded modelling paste quite thinly and cut out 2 large butterflies and 2 small butterflies, using the templates. Dust the work surface with a little more icing sugar and repeat with the dark blue modelling paste to make eight butterflies in total. Cut each butterfly in half vertically and transfer the wings to the prepared tray.

3 Spoon the royal icing into the piping bag and pipe the outline of the wings onto each butterfly. (For tips on piping, see pages 157–9.) Roll up the piping bag and store in an airtight container until needed. Leave the outlined butterfly wings to dry, overnight, uncovered, in a cool, dry place.

4 When the sugar paste and butterfly wings have dried, crease the sheet of card along the long edge into 3 concertina folds to make a deep v-shaped "trough" – this will help you to assemble the butterflies and allow the wings to dry at an angle. Cut out a 60 x 10cm/24 x 4in strip of baking parchment, then fold it in half along the long edge and use it to line the centre of the "trough". To assemble the large butterflies, pipe a 3cm/1¼in line of royal icing along the bottom crease of the "trough". Take one set of large butterfly wings and gently press the cut-side of each one into the icing to create a butterfly (for tips, see page 116). Starting at the tail end, pipe a second line of royal icing along the centre of the butterfly for the body and finish with a large dot of icing for the head (see picture). Repeat with the remaining large butterflies. To assemble the small butterflies, pipe 1.5cm/⅝in lines of royal icing along the bottom crease and repeat as above. Roll up the piping bag and store in an airtight container until needed. Leave the butterflies to dry in the "trough" for at least 2 hours.

5 When the assembled butterflies are stable and completely dry, carefully attach one large and one small butterfly to the top of each cake, securing them with a dot of royal icing. Leave the cakes for at least 10–15 minutes, uncovered, in a cool, dry place to allow the icing to set.

Santa's Sleigh Cake

MAKES 1 CAKE
50g/1¾oz apricot jam, warmed
18cm/7in round Fruit Cake
  (see pages 108–9)
icing sugar, for dusting
750g/1lb 10oz marzipan
765g/1lb 11oz white sugar paste
  (see pages 160–1)
100g/3½oz red-coloured
  modelling paste (see pages
  160–1)
10g/¼oz each of green-, dark
  pink-, lilac-, orange- and pale
  yellow-coloured sugar pastes
  or brightly coloured sugar
  pastes of your choice (see
  pages 160–1)
50g/1¾oz white soft-peak
  Royal Icing (see page 46)

YOU WILL NEED
pastry brush
18cm/7in round cake drum
small rolling pin
5mm/¼in marzipan spacers
  (optional)
sleigh templates (see page 169)
sharp knife
small offset palette knife
tray lined with baking
  parchment
ruler
piping bag fitted with a no. 1.5
  plain nozzle
60cm/2ft red satin ribbon,
  3.5cm/1⅓in wide

TIP
You will need to cover the cake in
marzipan the day before you want
to cover it with sugar paste.

1 Brush the top of the cake drum with a little jam, then attach the cake to the drum, upside-down, to give the cake a flat top. Dust the work surface with a little icing sugar, then knead the marzipan until it is soft, but take care not to overknead it. Fill any gaps around the base of the cake with a little of the kneaded marzipan. Following the instructions on page 153, cover the cake with the remaining kneaded marzipan, followed the next day by 750g/1lb 10oz of kneaded white sugar paste. Leave the sugar paste covered cake overnight, uncovered, in a cool, dry place to allow the sugar paste to dry.

2 Dust the work surface with a little icing sugar, then knead the red modelling paste until it is soft and pliable. Roll out the kneaded modelling paste until it is 5mm/¼in thick, using marzipan spacers if you like. Place the templates for the front, back and side panels of the sleigh on the rolled modelling paste and cut around them with the sharp knife. You will need 1 front panel, 1 back panel and 2 side panels. Smooth the edges of each panel with your fingers. Using the offset palette knife, transfer the panels to the prepared tray, taking care not to stretch or pull the modelling paste.

3 To make the sleigh's skis, dust the work surface with a little more icing sugar, then knead the remaining white sugar paste until it is soft and pliable. Divide the sugar paste into two balls, then roll each one into a long, thin sausage about 13cm/5in long. Flatten the sausages slightly, then curl the ends of each one back on itself (see picture). For the presents, knead each of the brightly coloured sugar pastes until soft and pliable. Mould the kneaded sugar pastes into 10 different 3D-shapes such as cubes and spheres. Transfer the skis and presents to the prepared tray. Leave the sleigh panels, skis and presents to dry overnight, uncovered, in a cool, dry place.

4 When the sugar paste and decorations have dried, spoon the royal icing into the piping bag. Pipe the ribbon details onto each present, then pipe the swirl design on the top of the sleigh side panels (see picture). (For tips on piping, see pages 157–9.) Leave the icing to set for 10–15 minutes. Meanwhile, wrap the ribbon around the base of the cake, securing the join at the back with a little royal icing and trimming as necessary. Pipe small dots of royal icing just above the top of the ribbon, evenly spacing them around the cake (see picture).

5 To assemble the sleigh, pipe a line of royal icing along the side edges of the front and back sleigh panels, then gently press the side panels into position. Hold the sleigh in place for a few seconds while the icing sets, then support the panels with drinking glasses and leave to dry for at least 1 hour, uncovered, in a cool, dry place. Roll up the piping bag and store in an airtight container until needed. When the sleigh is stable, carefully place it in the centre of the cake, securing it with a little royal icing. Attach the skis to the cake along the base of the sleigh, then place the presents inside, securing each element with royal icing. Leave to set, uncovered, in a cool, dry place, before serving.

Fruit Cake

The table opposite shows you the quantity of ingredients and baking times required for different cake sizes and styles. It also offers advice on serving portions. Simply select your size and style and follow the method below.

dates
prunes
dried apricots
sultanas
raisins
currants
glacé cherries
orange zest
lemon zest
orange juice
lemon juice
brandy
salted butter
muscovado sugar
treacle
eggs
plain flour
baking powder
ground cinnamon
ground ginger
ground nutmeg
ground mixed spice
chopped glacé ginger
vanilla extract

YOU WILL NEED
cake tin lined with baking
  parchment (for tips on lining
  cake tins, see page 149)

TIP
The cake can be kept for up to
6 weeks to mature. Wrap it in a
double layer of baking parchment
and then in a layer of foil. Store
at room temperature in a cool,
dry place.

1 Snip the dates, prunes and apricots into thirds with kitchen scissors, then transfer to a large mixing bowl. Add the sultanas, raisins, currants, glacé cherries, orange and lemon zests and juices and brandy and mix well. Leave to steep, covered, for 6 hours or overnight at room temperature.

2 At the end of the steeping time, preheat the oven to 140°C/275°F/Gas 1. Put the butter and sugar in a saucepan over a low heat. Cook, stirring frequently, until the sugar has melted. Pour the mixture into a large mixing bowl, then add the treacle and eggs and mix well. Sift the flour, baking powder and spices into the bowl and fold in, using a metal spoon. Add the steeped fruits and their juices, then add the glacé ginger and vanilla extract and mix until well combined.

3 Spoon the mixture into the prepared cake tin, levelling the surface with the back of a metal spoon. Bake for the recommended time or until a skewer inserted into the centre comes out clean. As oven temperatures can vary, check on the cake about 5 minutes before the end of the recommended baking time.

4 Remove the cake from the oven and leave in the tin to cool completely. (For tips on covering the cake with marzipan and sugar paste, see page 153.)

Use this fruit cake recipe for the following recipes throughout this book:

Santa's Sleigh Cake
page 107

Hydrangea Cake
page 130

	10cm/4in round or square cake	13cm/5in round or square cake	15cm/6in round or square cake	18cm/7in round or square cake	20cm/8in round, square or heart cake	23cm/9in round or square cake
dates	20g/¾oz	30g/1oz/scant ¼ cup	45g/1½oz/¼ cup	70g/2½oz/heaped ⅓ cup	90g/3¼oz/scant ½ cup	120g/4¼oz/⅔ cup
prunes	20g/¾oz	30g/1oz	45g/1½oz/scant ¼ cup	70g/2½oz/scant ⅓ cup	90g/3¼oz/heaped ⅓ cup	120g/4¼oz/heaped ½ cup
dried apricots	20g/¾oz	30g/1oz/ scant ¼ cup	45g/1½oz/¼ cup	70g/2½oz/heaped ⅓ cup	90g/3¼oz/½ cup	120g/4¼oz/⅔ cup
sultanas	60g/2¼oz/½ cup	80g/2¾oz/scant ⅔ cup	115g/4oz/scant 1 cup	180g/6¼oz/scant 1½ cups	230g/8½oz/ scant 2 cups	300g/10½oz/2½ cups
raisins	60g/2¼oz/½ cup	80g/2¾oz/scant ⅔ cup	115g/4oz/scant 1 cup	180g/6¼oz/scant 1½ cups	230g/8½oz/scant 2 cups	300g/10½oz/ 2½ cups
currants	75g/2½oz/ ½ cup	100g/3½oz/⅔ cup	150g/5½oz/ 1 cup	225g/8oz/1½ cups	300g/10½oz/ 2 cups	400g/14oz/ 2⅔ cups
glacé cherries	50g/1¾oz	70g/2½oz	100g/3½oz	150g/5½oz	200g/7oz	265g/9¼oz
orange zest	½ orange	1 orange	1 orange	1½ oranges	2 oranges	2½ oranges
lemon zest	½ lemon	1 lemon	1 lemon	1½ lemons	2 lemons	2½ lemons
orange juice	1 tbsp	1 tbsp	1 tbsp	2 tbsp	2 tbsp	2–3 tbsp
lemon juice	1 tbsp	1 tbsp	2 tbsp	2 tbsp	2 tbsp	2–3 tbsp
brandy	3 tbsp	70ml/2¼fl oz/ generous ¼ cup	100ml/3½fl oz/ generous ⅓ cup	150ml/5fl oz/scant ⅔ cup	200ml/7fl oz/scant 1 cup	265ml/9½fl oz/ generous 1 cup
salted butter	60g/2¼oz	80g/2¾oz	125g/4½oz	190g/6¾oz	250g/9oz	330g/11¾oz
muscovado sugar	65g/2½oz/heaped ⅓ cup	90g/3¼oz/scant ½ cup	130g/4½oz/heaped ⅔ cup	195g/6¾oz/heaped 1 cup	260g/9¼oz/ heaped 1⅓ cups	350g/12oz/scant 2 cups
treacle	1½ tsp	1½ tsp	1 tbsp	1 tbsp	1 tbsp	2 tbsp
eggs	2 medium	2 medium	3 medium	4 medium	5 large	7 medium
plain flour	60g/2¼oz/ ½ cup	80g/2¾oz/scant ⅔ cup	120g/4¼oz/ scant 1 cup	180g/6¼oz/scant 1½ cups	240g/8½oz/scant 2 cups	320g/11¼oz/ heaped 2½ cups
baking powder	¼ tsp	¼ tsp	¼ tsp	½ tsp	½ tsp	¾ tsp
ground cinnamon	¼ tsp	¼ tsp	¾ tsp	1¼ tsp	1½ tsp	2 tsp
ground ginger	¼ tsp	¼ tsp	¾ tsp	1¼ tsp	1½ tsp	2 tsp
ground nutmeg	¼ tsp	¼ tsp	¾ tsp	1¼ tsp	1½ tsp	2 tsp
ground mixed spice	¼ tsp	¼ tsp	¾ tsp	1¼ tsp	1½ tsp	2 tsp
chopped glacé ginger	10g/¼oz	15g/½oz	20g/¾oz	30g/1oz	40g/1½oz	50g/1¾oz/scant ¼ cup
vanilla extract	¼ tsp	¼ tsp	¼ tsp	½ tsp	½ tsp	¾ tsp
baking time	1¼ hours	1½ hours	2 hours	2¼ hours	2½ hours	2¾ hours
serves	10	12	15–20	20–30	30–40	40–50

Baby Shower Cupcakes

MAKES 6 CUPCAKES
icing sugar, for dusting
150g/5½oz blue-coloured
**   modelling paste (see pages**
**   160–1)**
60g/2¼oz cream-coloured sugar
**   paste (see pages 160–1)**
10g/¼oz black-coloured sugar
**   paste (see pages 160–1)**
150g/5½oz pink-coloured
**   modelling paste (see pages**
**   160–1)**
edible glue or cooled, boiled
**   water**
2 lengths of dried spaghetti,
**   each one cut into 3 small**
**   pieces (optional)**
½ recipe quantity Vanilla
**   Frosting (see page 118)**
6 Cupcakes in a flavour of your
**   choice (see page 129)**

YOU WILL NEED
ruler
small paintbrush
double-ended ball tool
design wheeler tool with stitch
**   head**
sharp knife
piping bag fitted with a
**   20mm/¾in closed-star nozzle**
6 cupcake wrappers

TIP
You will need to make the bears
and rabbits the day before they
are needed.

1 This recipe makes six cupcakes but if you only want to make one, simply decide whether you would like to make a bear or a rabbit and scale down the listed ingredients. Dust the work surface with a little icing sugar, then knead all of the modelling and sugar pastes until they are soft and pliable. Store the kneaded pastes in an airtight container until needed so they do not dry out and crack.

2 To make a teddy bear, dust the work surface with a little more icing sugar. For the bear's body, roll 20g/¾oz of the blue modelling paste into a teardrop shape. For the arms and legs, roll 10g/¼oz of the blue modelling paste into 4 balls. Roll each of the balls into tapered sausages about 4cm/1½in long, then slightly flatten the thicker ends to form paws. For the paw pads, roll 4 small pea-sized balls of cream sugar paste and attach them to the paws with edible glue, flattening them slightly as you do so. Using the picture as a guide, mould the legs and arms around the body, then attach with edible glue.

3 To make the head, roll 10g/¼oz of the blue modelling paste into a ball. For the ears, roll 2 pea-sized balls of blue modelling paste and indent the centre of each one with the small head of the ball tool. While the modelling paste is still soft, use the wheeler tool to indent "stitched" lines along the bear's body, arms, legs and head. Attach the head to the body using edible glue. Insert a piece of dried spaghetti into the bear's body to support the head and hold it in place, if necessary.

4 To make the muzzle, roll a pea-sized ball of cream sugar paste, then flatten it into an oval. Attach the ears and muzzle to the head with a little edible glue. For the nose, roll a small ball of blue modelling paste. Attach the nose to the muzzle with edible glue, flattening it slightly as you do so, then indent a line coming down from the nose with the sharp knife (see picture). For the eyes, roll 2 tiny balls of black sugar paste and attach with edible glue. Repeat steps 2–4 to make three bears.

5 To make a rabbit, repeat steps 2–4 above using pink modelling paste instead of blue. To make rabbit ears instead of bear ears, roll 2 pea-sized balls of pink modelling paste and 2 tiny balls of cream sugar paste and mould each one into a teardrop shape. Using edible glue, attach the cream teardrops to the centre of the pink teardrops. Attach the ears to the head with a little edible glue. Repeat to make three rabbits in total.

6 Leave the bears and rabbits to dry overnight, uncovered in a cool dry place. When the bears and rabbits have dried, spoon the frosting into the piping bag and pipe a high swirl (see page 157) onto each cupcake. (For tips on piping, see pages 157–9.) Put each cupcake in a cupcake wrapper, then place a bear or rabbit on top of each one, gently pressing them into the centre of the frosting swirl to hold them in place.

CHAPTER FOUR

With a little time and patience it's easy to make a range of stunning treats. Add the wow factor to any party with a Gift-Wrapped Cake. The Butterfly Fancies will be the talk of the tea party and your friends and family will be mad as hatters when they see the Teapot Cake. Everything looks too good to eat, but trust me, that won't stop anyone.

DECORATE
TO
IMPRESS

Ivory Corsage Wedding Cake

MAKES 1 CAKE
2 x 10cm/4in round Chocolate
   Sponge Cakes (see pages
   62–3)
2 x 20cm/8in round Chocolate
   Sponge Cakes (see pages
   62–3)
2 recipe quantities Chocolate
   Ganache (see page 16)
15cm/6in Rich Chocolate Cake
   (see pages 56–7)
icing sugar, for dusting
2kg/4lb 8oz ivory-coloured
   sugar paste (see pages 160–1)
200g/7oz ivory modelling
   paste (see pages 160–1)
edible glue
50g/1¾oz ivory-coloured stiff-
   peak Royal Icing (see page 46)

YOU WILL NEED
10cm/4in round cake drum
20cm/8in round cake drum
15cm/6in round cake drum
small rolling pin
small and large corsage
   templates (see page 165)
sharp knife
foam pad or a clean, dry folded
   kitchen towel
double-ended ball tool
indented foam pad or a piece
   of crinkled kitchen foil
small paintbrush
piping bag fitted with a no. 2
   plain nozzle
plastic dowels
1.5m/5ft ivory satin ribbon,
   15mm/⅝in wide
small and large leaf templates
   (see page 165)

TIP
You will need to make the
corsages at least a day before
they are needed. (For tips on
making corsages, see page 53).

1 Following the instructions on page 150 and using the cake drums as firm bases, layer the 10cm/4in cakes and the 20cm/8in chocolate sponge cakes, then fill with chocolate ganache to make one tall 10cm/4in cake and one tall 20cm/8in cake. Following the instructions on page 152, cover each tier of the cake with the remaining ganache. Chill in the fridge for at least 2 hours. When the ganache has set, dust the work surface with a little icing sugar, then knead 850g/1lb 14oz of the sugar paste until it is soft and pliable. Following the instructions on page 153, cover the 20cm/8in cake with the kneaded sugar paste. Repeat as above using 625g/1lb 6oz of sugar paste to cover the 15cm/6in cake and 425g/15oz to cover the 10cm/4in cake.

2 To make a corsage, dust the work surface with icing sugar and knead 30g/1oz of the modelling paste until it is soft and pliable. For the centre of the corsage, roll a blueberry-sized ball of modelling paste. Roll out the remaining kneaded paste quite thinly. Place the templates for the small and large flowers onto the rolled modelling paste and cut around them with the sharp knife. You will need 1 small flower and 2 large flowers. Place the flowers on the foam pad, then gently roll the large head of the ball tool over each petal to soften the edges. Place one of the large flowers on the indented foam pad. Brush a little edible glue in the centre of the large flower, then lay the other large flower over the top. Attach the central ball to the centre of the small flower, wrapping the petals of the flower around the ball, then attach it to the centre of the corsage – to achieve a closed-bud effect, secure the petals tightly to the ball with a little edible glue; to achieve an opened-bud effect, wrap the petals around the ball attaching them with a little edible glue at the base only. Making one corsage at a time, repeat with 120g/4¼oz of the modelling paste to make four corsages in total. Leave the cakes and corsages to dry overnight, uncovered, in a cool, dry place.

3 When the sugar paste and corsages have dried, spoon the royal icing into the piping bag. Following the instructions on page 156, stack the cakes on top of each other with plastic dowels. Wrap the ribbon around the base of each tier, securing the join at the back with a little royal icing and trimming as necessary. Position the corsages over the cake tiers and secure them in place with a little royal icing. Dust the work surface with a little icing sugar, then knead the remaining modelling paste until it is soft and pliable. Roll out the kneaded paste quite thinly. Assessing how many extra petals you will need to fill the gaps between the corsages and the cake, cut around the large flower template as many times as necessary, then cut each flower into 5 petals. Soften the edges of the petals as above in step 2. While the petals are still soft, attach them to the cake behind the corsage flowers to make four full corsages in total, securing each one in place with a little royal icing. Starting from the corsages, pipe 3 or 4 curvy lines onto the cake. Roll the modelling paste trimmings into a ball, then re-roll quite thinly and cut out 8 small leaves and 8 large leaves using the templates. Soften each leaf as above in step 2, then pinch together the base of each one to form an inward curve. Attach the leaves to the cake along the curvy piped lines, securing each one with a little royal icing. Leave the cake overnight, uncovered, in a cool, dry place to allow the icing to set.

Butterfly Fancies

MAKES 16 FANCIES
18cm/7in square Vanilla Sponge Cake (see pages 62–3), cooled
1 recipe quantity Vanilla Sugar Syrup (see page 119)
½ recipe quantity Vanilla Buttercream (see page 16)
2 heaped tbsp seedless raspberry jam
icing sugar, for dusting
175g/6oz marzipan
2 tbsp apricot jam
600g/1lb 5oz/heaped 4¾ cups fondant icing sugar
yellow food colouring paste
turquoise food colouring paste
green food colouring paste
lilac food colouring paste
50g/1¾oz white stiff-peak Royal Icing (see page 46)

YOU WILL NEED
16 foil cupcake cases
butterfly templates (see page 168)
A4 sheet of paper
tray
baking parchment
piping bag fitted with a no. 2 plain nozzle
4 x A4 sheets of stiff card
ruler
small offset palette knife

1 Following steps 1–4 on page 18, make 16 un-iced fancies. Following the instructions on page 151, cover one-quarter of the fancies in pale yellow, turquoise, green and lilac (not shown) fondant icings, then wrap in cupcake cases – mix up one batch of icing at a time according to the packet instructions. Leave the fancies to dry until the icing has set, then cover and store at room temperature until needed.

2 Trace 16 pairs of butterfly wings onto the sheet of paper. Place the sheet of paper on the tray and lay a sheet of baking parchment over the top – if you want to allow for breakages, trace about 20 pairs of wings onto the sheet of paper. Use masking tape or drinking glasses to hold the baking parchment in place – your piping may smudge if the baking parchment moves. Spoon the royal icing into the piping bag. Piping one wing at a time, carefully pipe over the outline of the wing, then pipe a random "lacework" pattern to completely cover the centre of the wing **(a)**. (For tips on piping, see pages 157–9.) Repeat until you have at least 32 piped wings in total. Leave to dry overnight, uncovered, in a cool, dry place. Roll up the piping bag and store in an airtight container until needed.

3 When the wings have dried, crease each sheet of card along the long edge into 3 concertina folds to make four v-shaped "troughs" – this will help you to assemble the butterflies and allow the wings to dry at an angle. Cut out 4 strips of baking parchment, each about 60 x 10cm/23¾ x 4in, then fold them in half along the long edge and use them to line the centre of the "troughs". To assemble a butterfly, pipe a 3cm/1¼in line of royal icing along the bottom crease of one of the "troughs". Carefully lift a pair of wings away from the baking parchment with the offset palette knife, then gently press each one into the icing to create a butterfly **(b)**. Starting at the tail end, pipe a second line of icing along the centre of the butterfly for the body and finish with a large dot of icing for the head **(c)**. Repeat with the remaining sets of butterfly wings to make 16 butterflies in total. Leave the butterflies to dry in the "troughs" for at least 2 hours. Roll up the piping bag and store in an airtight container until needed. When the butterflies are stable and completely dry, carefully attach them to the top of the fondant fancies, securing each one with a little royal icing. Leave the fancies for at least 10–15 minutes, uncovered, in a cool, dry place to allow the icing to set.

(a)

(b)

(c)

Basic Frosting

Frostings are piped onto cupcakes in decorative swirls to heighten their visual appeal and flavour. They have a much higher ratio of icing sugar to butter than buttercream and as a result, frosted swirls "air dry" on the outside but stay soft on the inside. Plain and vanilla frostings can be coloured with food colouring pastes. To colour frosting, simply add a small amount of food colouring paste to the mixture, using the end of a cocktail stick, and mix until combined. Repeat until the desired colour is achieved. (For tips on piping frosting swirls, see page 157.)

MAKES 350G/12OZ
250g/9oz/2 cups icing sugar
100g/3½oz salted butter,
**   softened**
1 tbsp milk
food colouring pastes (optional)

YOU WILL NEED
electric mixer
cocktail stick (optional)

For basic frosting, sift the icing sugar into a mixing bowl. Add the butter and beat with the electric mixer until combined. With the mixer running, gradually add the milk. When all the milk is incorporated, beat for 5 minutes until light and fluffy.

Variations

Chocolate Frosting: use 300g/10½oz/2½ cups icing sugar and 50g/1¾oz/scant ½ cup cocoa, sift into the bowl and beat with the butter as above. Use 3 tbsp milk and add to the mixture as above.
Citrus Frosting: beat in the finely grated zest of 1 small lemon or 1 small orange with the icing sugar and butter.
Coffee Frosting: beat in ½ tsp coffee extract with the icing sugar and butter.
Vanilla Frosting: beat in ½ tsp vanilla extract with the icing sugar and butter.

CREAM CHEESE FROSTING

MAKES 480G/1LB 1OZ
300g/10½oz/2½ cups icing
**   sugar**
50g/1¾oz salted butter,
**   softened**
130g/4½oz chilled cream cheese

YOU WILL NEED
electric mixer

Sift the icing sugar into a mixing bowl. Add the butter and beat with the electric mixer until combined. Add all of the cream cheese, then beat for about 5 minutes until light and fluffy, take care not to overmix as the frosting will become too runny.

Use these frosting recipes for the following recipes throughout this book:

Chocolate Swirl
Mini Cupcakes
page 15

Rose Swirl
Cupcakes
page 22

Rose Bouquet
Cupcakes
page 67

Chocolate Heart
Cake Pops
page 68

Baby Shower
Cupcakes
page 110

Flower Cake Pops
page 132

Sugar Syrups

Lightly brushing sponge cakes with a little sugar syrup will keep them moist and also adds extra flavour. Take care not to use too much, as it can make cakes overly sweet. Use it with any of the recipes listed below. To keep your cakes and cupcakes as delicious as they look, I highly recommend brushing a little sugar syrup over any sponge cake you plan to cover and decorate over a 3–4 day period.

MAKES 1 RECIPE QUANTITY
100g/3½oz/scant ½ cup caster sugar

Put the sugar and 100ml/3½fl oz/scant ½ cup water in a saucepan and bring to the boil, without stirring. Leave to cool a little, then flavour, if you like (see below). Any leftover syrup can be kept in a sealed container in the fridge for 2 weeks.

Flavours

Citrus: replace the water with 100ml/3½fl oz/scant ½ cup freshly squeezed orange or lemon juice.
Coffee: add 1 tbsp coffee extract with the water.
Coffee Liqueur: add 1 tbsp each of coffee extract and Amaretto or Tia Maria with the water.
Lemon Liqueur: replace the water with 100ml/3½fl oz/scant ½ cup freshly squeezed lemon juice and add 1 tbsp Grand Marnier or limoncello
Vanilla: add 1½ tsp vanilla extract with the water.

Use this sugar syrup recipe for the following recipes throughout this book:

Fresh Flower Fondant Fancies
page 18

Mini Ghost Cakes
page 91

Festive Ball Cakes
page 92

Christmas Pudding Cake
page 97

Butterfly Fancies
page 116

Teapot Cake
page 122

Magnificent Mini Cakes

MAKES 4 MINI CAKES
icing sugar, for dusting
600g/1lb 5oz white sugar paste
(see pages 160–1)
4 prepared Sponge or Marble
Round Mini Cakes (see page
128)
120g/4¼oz white flower paste
(see pages 160–1)
50g/1¾oz white soft-peak Royal
Icing (see page 46)
50g/1¾oz pale green-coloured
soft-peak Royal Icing (see
page 46)

YOU WILL NEED
small rolling pin
5mm/¼in marzipan spacers
(optional)
sharp knife
ruler
swirly design (see page 169)
baking parchment
pins
scriber or sharp needle
2 piping bags, each fitted with a
no. 2 plain nozzle

TIP
Always leave the sugar paste
covered cakes to dry overnight
before you start scribing them.
This makes it far less likely that
you will accidently indent the
sugar paste when decorating.

1 Dust the work surface with a little icing sugar, then knead the white sugar paste until it is soft and pliable. Roll out the kneaded sugar paste until it is 5mm/¼in thick, using marzipan spacers if you like. Cut out 4 squares, each measuring 13 x 13cm/5 x 5in. Following the instructions on page 153, use one square of sugar paste to cover each cake.

2 Knead 30g/1oz of the flower paste until it is smooth and elastic. Following steps 1–3 on page 126, make a small open rose. Repeat with the remaining flower paste to make four small roses in total. Leave the cakes and the roses overnight, uncovered, in a cool, dry place to allow the sugar and flower pastes to dry.

3 When the sugar and flower pastes have dried, trace the swirly design onto a sheet of baking parchment 4 times, then closely cut around the outline of each swirl to make 4 scribing guides. Cut out 4 circles of baking parchment that are slightly larger than the base of each cake. Carefully place the cakes on top of the parchment circles – this will make the cakes easier to turn when decorating.

4 Using the picture as a guide, position one of the scribing guides over the cake. Secure the guide in place with a couple of pins, pushing them through the top and bottom points of the swirl design – if the guide moves during scribing, the swirly design will be messy and hard to pipe over. Lightly prick the outline of the swirly design onto the cake with the scriber. (For tips on scribing, see page 83.) Scribe another 3 swirly designs onto the cake, evenly spacing the designs around the side. Repeat with the remaining cakes, using a new scribing guide for each one.

5 Spoon the white and pale green soft-peak royal icings into the piping bags. Using the indentations made by the scriber as a guide, pipe a line of white soft-peak royal icing from the top of the cake to the centre of the swirly design, then carefully pipe over the details of the swirl. (For tips on piping, see pages 157–9.) Repeat until all the swirly designs have been piped over.

6 Spacing the lines evenly between the piped swirls, pipe 4 vertical lines of white soft-peak royal icing down the side of each cake – starting from the top and finishing with a small dot of icing at the base. Repeat with the pale green soft-peak royal icing, piping 2 vertical lines of green icing down each side of the vertical white lines. Pipe a small dot of pale green soft-peak royal icing in the centre of each swirly design. Leave the cakes for 1 hour, uncovered, in a cool, dry place to allow the icing to set. Roll up the piping bags and store in an airtight container until needed.

7 When the icing has dried, attach a flower paste rose to the top of each cake, securing them in place with a dot of white soft-peak royal icing.

Teapot Cake

MAKES 1 CAKE
2 x 15cm/6in Mocha Sponge ball
   cake halves (see pages 62–3)
1 recipe quantity Vanilla
   Buttercream (see page 16)
1 recipe quantity Sugar Syrup
   (see page 119)
icing sugar, for dusting
325g/11½oz ivory-coloured or
   white modelling paste (see
   pages 160–1)
1.3kg/3lb ivory-coloured or
   white sugar paste (see pages
   160–1)
white soft-peak Royal Icing
   (see page 46)
20g/¾oz dark blue-coloured
   sugar paste (see pages 160–1)
1 tbsp cocoa butter beans
dark blue, light blue, white and
   green edible food dusts

YOU WILL NEED
serrated knives
sharp knife
pastry brush
rolling pins
5mm/¼in marzipan spacers
   (optional)
ruler
tray lined with baking
   parchment
double-ended ball tool
short plastic dowel
tissue paper
polystyrene ball about
   8cm/3¼in in diameter or
   tennis ball
icing smoother
15cm/6in round cake drum
50cm/20in ivory ribbon,
   8mm/⅜in wide
double-sided tape
piping bag fitted with a no. 2
   plain nozzle
paintbrushes

1 Using a long serrated knife, level the flat-side of the ball cake halves to ensure they will create a neat ball shape when sandwiched together. Take one of the ball cake halves and cut off the domed top **(a)**, then turn the cake cut-side down – this will form a flat, stable base for the bottom of the teapot. Place the domed ball cake on top to create a ball shape. Using a small serrated knife, trim off the top of the dome to create a level surface – this will form a flat, stable base for the teapot lid.

2 Using a long serrated knife, slice each cake in half horizontally to form four layers. Stack the layers back together and, if necessary, carefully trim the edge of the sponge with the sharp knife to neaten the ball cake and create a smooth, flat surface **(b)**. Following the instructions on page 92, fill and cover the cake with buttercream, lightly brushing the top of each layer with sugar syrup. Chill in the fridge for 2 hours until set.

3 Meanwhile, dust the work surface with a little icing sugar, then knead the ivory modelling paste until it is soft and pliable. For the base of the teapot lid, roll out 150g/5½oz of the ivory modelling paste until it is 5mm/¼in thick, using marzipan spacers if you like. Cut out one circle about 10cm/4in diameter and one circle about 8cm/3¼in in diameter. To make the tip of the teapot lid, mould 5g/⅛oz of the ivory modelling paste into a teardrop shape. Place the teapot lid pieces on the prepared tray.

4 To make the teapot handle, roll 30g/1oz of the ivory modelling paste into a long sausage about 15cm/6in long, then flatten the handle with the rolling pin until it is about 5mm/¼in thick. Round the ends of the handle with your fingers for a neat finish. Lay the handle on its side on the prepared tray and curve it into the desired shape (see picture on page 125).

5 For the spout, roll 50g/1¾oz of ivory modelling paste into a long, tapered sausage about 10cm/4in long. Flatten the wider end of the sausage to form the base of the spout, then indent a hole in the other end with the large head of the ball tool for the tip of the spout. Curve the modelling paste into

(a)

(b)

a spout shape. Using the dowel, indent a small hole at the base of the spout – this will help you to attach the spout to the cake (see j). Remove the dowel and leave to one side until needed. Place the spout on the prepared tray and use some crumpled tissue paper to keep it in position while it dries.

6 To make the dome of the teapot lid, roll out the remaining ivory modelling paste until it is 5mm/¼in thick, using marzipan spacers if you like, then cut out a circle about 11cm/4¼in in diameter. Cover the polystyrene ball with cling film, then lay the modelling paste over the top, smoothing down the sides with your hands **(c)** – this forms the concave dome when dry **(d)**. Place the polystyrene ball in the top of a drinking glass to keep the modelling paste in position while it dries. Leave all of the teapot lid pieces to dry overnight, uncovered, in a cool, dry place.

7 When the buttercream has set, remove the cake from the fridge. Dust the work surface with a little icing sugar, then knead 1kg/2lb 4oz of the ivory sugar paste until it is soft and pliable. Roll out the kneaded sugar paste until it is 5mm/¼in thick, using marzipan spacers if you like. Lift the rolled sugar paste and gently place it over the top of the cake, taking care not to stretch or pull it, then use your hands to smooth it over the top and side of the cake. Trim off any excess sugar paste at the base of the cake, leaving about a 2cm/¾in border. Gently ease the border under the cake. Smooth the sugar paste again using the icing smoother. Decide which section of the cake will be the front, then concentrate on making that section look as smooth and neat as possible, hiding any creases in the sugar paste at the back of the cake.

8 Dust the work surface with a little more icing sugar, then knead the remaining ivory sugar paste until it is soft and pliable. Following the instructions on page 154, cover the cake drum with sugar paste and line the edge with ivory ribbon, trimming as necessary and securing the join at the back with double-sided tape. Leave the covered cake and cake drum overnight, uncovered, in a cool, dry place to allow the sugar paste to dry.

(c)

(d)

9 The next day, spoon the royal icing into the piping bag. To assemble the lid, attach the small base circle to the centre of the large base circle **(e)** with royal icing. (For tips on piping, see pages 157–9.) Turn the base upside-down and attach the dome to the centre of the larger circle with royal icing **(f)**. Dust the work surface with a little icing sugar, then knead the dark blue sugar paste until it is soft and pliable. Roll the sugar paste into a long thin sausage about 10cm/4in long. Attach the blue trim around the base of the dome **(g)** with a little royal icing. Trim as necessary. Attach the teardrop tip to the centre of the dome and secure in place with royal icing. Leave the lid to firm up a little.

10 Put the cocoa butter beans in the centre of a plate set over a bowl of just-boiled water. Put a small amount of the edible food dusts around the edge of the plate, then mix with some of the melting beans to make an edible painter's palette. Using the picture as a guide, paint a floral pattern over the cake **(h)**. Leave to one side for about 20 minutes until the pattern has dried.

11 Attach the handle to the cake with royal icing, then hold it in place for a few seconds while the icing sets **(i)**. Insert the dowel into the indent in the base of the spout. Position the spout at the front of the cake, then push the dowel into the cake at a slight angle **(j)** and secure the spout in place with royal icing. Use crumpled pieces of tissue paper to support the handle and spout while they dry. Attach the lid to the top of the cake with royal icing. Allow the icing to set completely before serving.

(e)   **(f)**   **(g)**

(h)   **(i)**   **(j)**

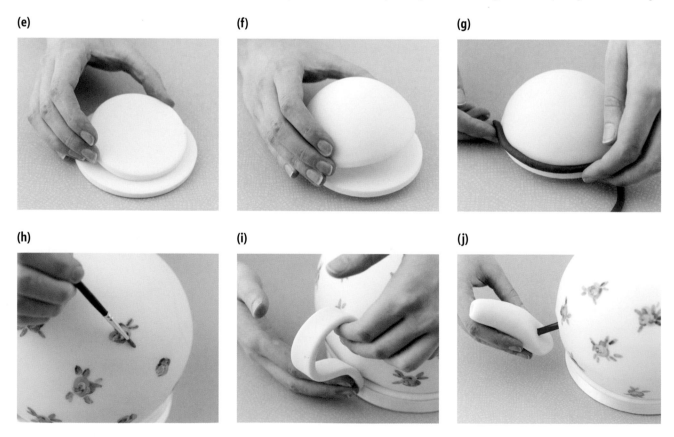

Rose Cupcakes

MAKES 6 CUPCAKES
icing sugar, for dusting
330g/11¾oz white flower paste
(see pages 160–1)
edible glue or cooled, boiled
water
pink edible food dust
¼ recipe quantity Vanilla
buttercream (see page 16)
6 Vanilla or Citrus Cupcakes
(see page 129)

YOU WILL NEED
small rolling pin
small, medium and large rose
petal templates (see page 168)
or 2.5cm/1in, 3.5cm/1¹⁄₃in and
4cm/1½in rose petal cutters
sharp knife
foam pad or a clean, dry folded
kitchen towel
double-ended ball tool
small paintbrushes
cocktail stick

TIPS
You can make small or large roses
to decorate your cupcakes or a
mixture of both. Always take care
not to flatten the curved shape
of the medium and large petals
when attaching them to the roses.
If necessary, support the outer
petals of large roses while they
dry with pieces of crumpled tissue
paper or foil.

Always use dry edible food dust
when colouring delicate flowers.

1 Dust the work surface with a little icing sugar, then knead 30g/1oz of the flower paste until smooth and elastic. Mould 5g/⅛oz of the kneaded paste into a cone shape. Repeat to make six cones in total. Leave the cones to dry overnight, uncovered, in a cool, dry place.

2 When the cones have dried, dust the work surface with icing sugar, then knead 50g/1¾oz of the flower paste until it is smooth and elastic. Roll out the kneaded flower paste quite thinly. Place the template for the small rose petal on the rolled flower paste and cut around it with the sharp knife to make 6 petals. Place the petals on the foam pad, then gently roll the large head of the ball tool over each petal to soften the edges. Lightly cover the back of the first petal with edible glue, then wrap it around one of the cones to form a tight bud **(a)**. Brush the bottom half of the second petal with edible glue. Attach one side of the petal to the bud, leaving the other side unattached and slightly hanging away from the bud. Brush the bottom half of the third petal with a little edible glue. Slightly tuck one side of the third petal under the second. Gently smooth the overlap with your finger and leave the other side of the third petal unattached and slightly hanging away from the bud. Repeat with the remaining 3 petals, attaching both sides of the final petal to the bud, to form a rose bud.

3 For a small open rose, re-roll the flower paste trimmings quite thinly and cut out 9 petals with the medium rose petal template. Place the petals on the foam pad. Gently roll the ball tool over the centre of each one to give them a curved shape, then carefully curl the top edges outwards with the side of the cocktail stick. Following the instructions in step 2, attach the petals to the rose bud **(b)**.

4 For a large open rose, re-roll the flower paste trimmings quite thinly and cut out 6 petals using the large rose petal template. Following the instructions in steps 2 and 3, attach the petals to the small rose.

5 Repeat steps 2–4 with the remaining flower paste to make six roses in total. Leave the roses to dry overnight, uncovered, at room temperature. When the roses have dried, brush the centre of each one with a little pink edible food dust. Following the instructions on page 152, spread a thin layer of buttercream over the top of each cupcake, then carefully place a rose on top of each one.

(a)

(b)

Mini Cakes

MAKES 4 MINI CAKES
10cm/4in square Rich Chocolate, Sponge or Marble Cake (see pages 56–7, 62–3 or 76–7)
1 recipe quantity Sugar Syrup (see page 119)
½ recipe quantity Vanilla Buttercream or Chocolate Ganache (see page 16)

YOU WILL NEED
cake leveller or small serrated knife
5cm/2in circle cutter
pastry brush
small offset palette knife
4 x 5cm/2in round cake cards

PREPARING ROUND MINI CAKES

Chill the cake in the fridge for at least 1 hour until cold and firm. Using the cake leveller, level the top of the cake, then slice it in half horizontally. From each layer, stamp out 4 circles using the 5cm/2in circle cutter, to make 8 sponge circles. Lightly brush the top of half of the sponge circles with sugar syrup, then spread a thin layer of buttercream over the top with the offset palette knife. Carefully place the plain sponge circles on top of the filling to make four sandwiched mini cakes in total. (For tips on layering and filling cakes, see page 150.) Attach the mini cakes to the cake cards with a little buttercream. Following the instructions on page 152, cover the cakes with buttercream, then chill in the fridge for 2 hours until set. When the buttercream has set, the cakes will be ready to be covered in sugar paste.

MAKES 4 MINI CAKES
4 x 8cm/3¼in Sponge or Marble ball cake halves (see pages 62–3, 76–7)
1 recipe quantity Sugar Syrup (see page 119)
½ recipe quantity Vanilla Buttercream (see page 16)
4 tsp seedless raspberry jam

YOU WILL NEED
small serrated knife
pastry brush
small offset palette knife
4 x 8cm/3¼in round cake cards

TIP
For tips on baking ball cake halves, see page 92.

PREPARING DOME MINI CAKES

Level the flat-side of one of the ball cake halves with the serrated knife, then slice it in half horizontally to form two layers. Lightly brush the top of the flat layer with sugar syrup, then spread a thin layer of buttercream followed by a thin layer of jam over the top of each one with the offset palette knife. Carefully place the domed layer of the cake on top of the filling to form a domed sandwich. Repeat with the remaining ball cake halves to make four layered dome cakes in total. (For tips on layering and filling cakes, see page 150.) Attach the dome cakes to the cake cards with a little buttercream. Following the instructions on page 152, cover the cakes with buttercream, then chill in the fridge for 2 hours until set. When the buttercream has set, the cakes will be ready to be covered in sugar paste.

Use this round mini cake recipe for the following recipe:

Magnificent Mini Cakes
page 121

Use this dome mini cake recipe for the following recipe:

Birthday Butterfly Mini Domes
page 104

Cupcakes

MAKES 6 OR 12 CUPCAKES OR 24 MINI CUPCAKES
Rich Chocolate, Sponge or Marble Cake mixture for 6 or 12 cupcakes or 24 mini cupcakes (see pages 56–7, 62–3 or 76–7)

YOU WILL NEED
12-cup muffin tin or 24-cup mini muffin tin
6 or 12 cupcake cases or 24 mini cupcake cases

TIP
Remember you can make cupcakes with a flavoured basic sponge cake mixture too (see pages 62–3).

1 Preheat the oven to 180°C/350°F/Gas 4 and arrange 6 or 12 paper cupcake cases in the 12-cup muffin tin or 24 mini cupcake cases in the 24-cup mini muffin tin. Divide your cake mixture evenly into the cupcake cases, filling each one about two-thirds full – to allow room for the cupcakes to rise.

2 Bake for the recommended time specified in the table for your chosen cake mixture or until the top of the cakes spring back slightly when gently pressed with a finger and a skewer inserted into the centre comes out clean.

3 Remove the cakes from the oven and leave to cool for 5 minutes, then remove from the tin, transfer to a wire rack and leave to cool completely. (For tips on covering cupcakes with buttercream, see page 152. For tips on icing cupcakes with frosted swirls, see page 157.)

Use this cupcake recipe for the following recipes throughout this book:

Chocolate Swirl Mini Cupcakes
page 15

Rose Swirl Cupcakes
page 22

Rose Bouquet Cupcakes
page 67

Mini Ghost Cakes
page 91

Baby Shower Cupcakes
page 110

Rose Cupcakes
page 126

Hydrangea Cake

MAKES 1 CAKE
50g/1¾oz apricot jam, warmed
20cm/8in round Fruit Cake
  (see pages 108–9)
icing sugar, for dusting
850g/1lb 14oz marzipan
950g/2lb 2oz white sugar
  paste (see pages 160–1)
pale green edible food dust
green edible food dust
50g/1¾oz white soft-peak
  Royal Icing (see page 46))

YOU WILL NEED
pastry brush
20cm/8in round cake drum
rolling pin
hydrangea cutter and veining
  mould set
indented foam pad or a piece of
  crinkled kitchen foil
small paintbrushes
piping bag fitted with a no. 1.5
  plain nozzle
25cm/10in ivory ribbon,
  5cm/2in wide

TIPS
You will need to cover the cake in marzipan the day before you want to cover it with sugar paste.

You will need to cover the cake in sugar paste and make and mould the hydrangea flowers at least a day before they are needed.

Always use dry edible food dust when colouring delicate flowers.

1 Brush the top of the cake drum with a little jam, then attach the cake to the drum, upside-down, to give the cake a flat top. Dust the work surface with a little icing sugar, then knead the marzipan until it is soft, but take care not to overknead it. Fill any gaps around the base of the cake with a little of the kneaded marzipan. Following the instructions on page 153, cover the cake with the remaining kneaded marzipan, followed the next day by 850g/1lb 14oz of kneaded white sugar paste. Leave the sugar paste covered cake overnight, uncovered, in a cool, dry place to allow the sugar paste to dry.

2 Dust the work surface with a little more icing sugar, then knead the remaining white sugar paste until it is soft and pliable. Roll out the kneaded sugar paste quite thinly. Stamp out a hydrangea using the hydrangea cutter, then immediately place it into the veining mould and gently bring the sides of the mould together. Place the veined hydrangea flower on the indented foam pad – this will help the flower to keep its curved shape as it dries. Stamping and moulding one hydrangea at a time, repeat with the remaining sugar paste to make 50 flowers in total, re-rolling the sugar paste as necessary. Leave the flowers to dry overnight, uncovered, in a cool, dry place.

3 When the sugar paste has set and the flowers have dried, brush the centre of each flower with pale green edible food dust, then brush a tiny amount of green edible food dust over the top in the very centre of the flower. Spoon the royal icing into the piping bag and pipe a small dot of icing in the centre of each flower. Leave the flowers for at least 2 hours, uncovered, in a cool, dry place to allow the icing to set.

4 Meanwhile, wrap the ribbon around the base of the cake, securing the join at the back with a little royal icing and trimming as necessary. Leave to dry completely. Roll up the piping bag and store in an airtight container until needed.

5 When the flowers have dried, attach the flowers in a random fashion over the top and side of the cake, securing each one with a dot of royal icing.

Flower Cake Pops

MAKES 12 CAKE POPS
icing sugar, for dusting
30g/1oz yellow-coloured sugar
    paste (see pages 160–1)
60g/2¼oz white sugar paste
    (see pages 160–1)
20g/¾oz white soft-peak Royal
    Icing (see page 46)
20g/¾oz pale green-coloured
    soft-peak Royal Icing (see
    page 46)
20g/¾oz yellow-coloured soft-
    peak royal icing (see page 46)
15cm/6in Basic Sponge Cake
    (see pages 62–3)
½ recipe quantity Vanilla
    Frosting (see page 118)
250g/9oz yellow candy coating
    buttons

YOU WILL NEED
small rolling pin
1.2cm/½in blossom plunger
    cutter
2cm/¾in daisy plunger cutter
foam pad or a clean, dry folded
    kitchen towel
3 piping bags
tray lined with baking
    parchment
12 paper lollipop sticks
3.5m/11½ft multi-coloured
    ribbon, 1cm/¼in wide, cut into
    12 equal lengths (optional)

TIP
You will need to make the sugar
paste flowers and the sponge cake
for the moist cake mix at least a
day before they are needed.

1 To make the small blossom flowers, dust the work surface with a little icing sugar, then knead the yellow sugar paste until it is soft and pliable. Roll out the kneaded sugar paste quite thinly and stamp out 36 small blossoms using the 1.2cm/½in blossom plunger cutter. Repeat with 30g/1oz of the white sugar paste to make 72 blossoms in total. To make the daisies, dust the work surface with a little more icing sugar, then knead the remaining white sugar paste until it is soft and pliable. Roll out the kneaded sugar paste quite thinly and stamp out 36 daisies using the 2cm/¾in daisy plunger cutter. Carefully transfer the blossoms and the daisies to the foam pad and leave to dry overnight, uncovered, in a cool, dry place.

2 When the flowers have dried, spoon the white soft-peak royal icing into one of the piping bags, then snip off the tip if necessary. Pipe a dot of icing in the centre of the small yellow blossoms. Repeat with the remaining soft peak royal icings and pipings bags, piping a dot of pale green icing into the centre of the small white blossoms and a dot of yellow icing into the centre of the daisies. Leave the flowers for at least 2 hours, uncovered, in a cool, dry place to allow the icing to set.

3 When the icing has set, follow the instructions in step 1 on page 68 and make a moist cake mixture using the sponge cake and frosting. Roll about 35g/1¼oz of the mixture into a ball, smoothing the surface with your fingers, then transfer to the prepared tray. Repeat with the remaining mixture to make 12 cake pops in total. Chill the cake pops in the fridge for about 1 hour until firm. Alternatively, freeze the cake pops for about 15 minutes until hard.

4 Put the candy coating in a heatproof bowl and rest it over a saucepan of gently simmering water, making sure the bottom of the bowl does not touch the water. Heat, stirring occasionally, until melted. Alternatively, put the candy coating in a microwavable bowl and microwave, uncovered, on medium for 2 minutes until melted, stirring every 30 seconds to ensure the coating does not overheat. The candy coating should have a smooth pouring consistency similar to double cream.

5 Dip the tip of one of the lollipop sticks about 1cm/½in into the melted candy coating and gently push it into the base of one of the cake pops until the coated tip is hidden from view. Holding the end of the lollipop stick, gently twist the cake pop through the candy coating until it is completely coated, using a teaspoon to help if necessary. Lift the cake pop out of the candy coating, allowing any excess coating to fall back in to the bowl. Transfer the coated cake pop to a drinking glass to hold it upright. Working quickly before the coating hardens, attach 3 of each flower over the top of the coated cake pop and leave to set for at least 10–15 minutes. Repeat with the remaining lollipop sticks, cake pops, candy coating and sugar paste flowers until all the cake pops are coated and decorated, reheating the candy coating if necessary. When the candy coating has completely set, tie a ribbon around each lollipop stick and finish with a bow, if you like.

Gift-Wrapped Cake

MAKES 1 CAKE
2 x 15cm/6in square Marble
  Cakes (see pages 76–7)
300g/10½oz Basic Buttercream
  (see page 16)
icing sugar, for dusting
600g/1lb 5oz white sugar paste
  (see pages 160–1)
70g/2½oz white modelling
  paste (see pages 160–1)
edible glue or cooled, boiled
  water
30g/1oz orange-coloured soft-
  peak Royal Icing (see page 46)
A4 sugar paste transfer sheet
50g/1¾oz white soft-peak Royal
  Icing (see page 46)

YOU WILL NEED
15cm/6in square cake drum
small rolling pin
bow templates (see page 165)
sharp knife
design wheeler tool
tray lined with baking
  parchment
small paintbrush
tissue paper
1.5cm/⅝in and 2.5cm/1in
  primrose flower plunger
  cutters
indented foam pad or a piece of
  crinkled kitchen foil
2 piping bags, each fitted with a
  no. 2 plain nozzle
ruler

TIP
Sugar paste sheets are widely
available online in a variety of
designs and colours. You can even
draw your own design and send
it to a company that can transfer
it onto a sheet of sugar paste.

1 Following the instructions on page 150 and using the cake drum as a firm base, layer the cakes, then fill with buttercream to make one tall 15cm/6in cake. Following the instructions on page 152, cover the cake with the remaining buttercream. Chill in the fridge for 2 hours. When the buttercream has set, dust the work surface with a little icing sugar and knead the sugar paste until it is soft and pliable. Following the instructions on page 153, cover the cake with the kneaded sugar paste.

2 Dust the work surface with a little more icing sugar, then knead 50g/1¾oz of the modelling paste until it is soft and pliable and roll out quite thinly. Place the templates for the bow on top of the rolled modelling paste and cut around them with the sharp knife, then use the design wheeler tool to indent a "stitched" line along the edges of each strip. Transfer the pieces to the prepared tray. Pinch together the plain-end of each tailpiece, then mould the modelling paste to give the tailpieces a slight curve (see picture). Take one of the loop pieces and brush one of the short ends with a little edible glue, then fold it in half to form a loop, pinching it in slightly at the join. Repeat with the remaining loop piece to make 2 loops. Stuff the hollow of each loop with a small piece of crumpled tissue paper – this will keep the modelling paste in position while it dries. To assemble the bow, arrange the loops and tailpieces in position on the prepared tray, then mould the bow join over the top to hide the point where the pieces meet, securing the pieces in place with a little edible glue.

3 Dust the work surface with a little more icing sugar and knead the remaining modelling paste until it is soft and pliable. Roll out the kneaded modelling paste quite thinly, then stamp out 12 primrose flowers using the 1.5cm/⅝in primrose plunger cutter. Roll the trimmings into a ball and repeat with the 2.5cm/1in primrose plunger cutter to make 6 larger primrose flowers. Place all of the flowers on the indented foam pad – this will help the flowers to keep their curved shape as they dry. Leave the cake, bow and flowers overnight, uncovered, in a cool, dry place to allow the sugar and modelling pastes to dry.

4 The next day, spoon the orange soft-peak royal icing into one of the piping bags and pipe a dot of icing into the centre of each flower. Leave to one side to allow the icing to set. Meanwhile, cut the sugar paste transfer sheet into 4 strips, each one about 18 x 6cm/7 x 2½in. Peel off the plastic backing from one of the strips, carefully sliding the sharp knife between the sheet and the backing. Brush the back of the strip with edible glue and position it in the centre of one side of the cake. Lining it up squarely at the base, gently smooth it over the side and top of the cake – you'll need to work quickly or the strip will dry out and become brittle. Working with one strip at a time, repeat with the remaining strips and edible glue until all the strips meet in the middle to create a "ribbon-wrapped" effect. Spoon the white royal icing into the remaining piping bag, then pipe small dots of icing along the edges of each strip. Attach the bow to the top of the cake, then attach the primrose flowers randomly over the "ribbon", securing the elements in place with a little royal icing.

Daisy Chain Mouse Cake

MAKES 1 CAKE
2 x 10cm/4in round Marble
Cakes (see pages 76–7)
½ recipe quantity Vanilla
Buttercream (see page 16)
icing sugar, for dusting
400g/14oz pale green-coloured
sugar paste (see pages 160–1)
70g/2½oz white modelling
paste (see pages 160–1)
20g/¾oz pale pink-coloured
modelling paste (see pages
160–1)
20g/¾oz purple-coloured
modelling paste (see pages
160–1)
10g/¼oz dark green-coloured
modelling or sugar paste
(see pages 160–1)
10g/¼oz pale yellow-coloured
modelling or sugar paste
(see pages 160–1)
edible glue or cooled, boiled
water
length of dried spaghetti
(optional)
black food paste colouring

YOU WILL NEED
10cm/4in round cake drum
sharp knife
small rolling pin
6cm/2½in 6-petal flower cutter
small paintbrush
ruler
double-ended ball tool
(optional)
2cm/¾in daisy plunger cutter
indented foam pad or a piece
of crinkled kitchen foil
38cm/15in lilac ribbon,
7mm/³⁄₈in wide

TIP
You will need to make the cake,
the mouse and the daisies at least
a day before they are needed.

1 Following the instructions on page 150 and using the cake drum as a firm base, layer the cakes, then fill with buttercream to make one tall 10cm/4in cake. Following the instructions on page 152, cover the cake with the remaining buttercream. Chill in the fridge for 2 hours.

2 When the buttercream has set, remove the cake from the fridge. Dust the work surface with a little icing sugar, then knead the pale green sugar paste until it is soft and pliable. Following the instructions on page 153, cover the cake with the kneaded sugar paste.

3 Knead all of the modelling pastes until they are soft and pliable. To make the mouse's head, mould 8g/¼oz of the white modelling paste into a teardrop shape and leave to firm up a little. To make the feet, mould 2 pea-sized teardrop shapes of white modelling paste. Indent the toes with the sharp knife, then slightly flatten the back of the feet to make a flat base for the body to rest on. Leave the feet to dry overnight, uncovered, in a cool, dry place. To make the lower body, mould 30g/1oz of the white modelling paste into a teardrop shape, then flatten it slightly at the top and base.

4 For the skirt of the dress, roll out 15g/½oz of the pale pink modelling paste quite thinly and cut out a flower using the 6-petal flower cutter. Repeat using the same amount of purple modelling paste to make a purple flower. Using a small amount of edible glue to secure each layer, lay the pale pink flower over the top of the lower body **(a)**, followed by the purple flower.

5 For the upper body, roll 5g/⅛oz of the white modelling paste into an oval, then gently press the top to flatten slightly. Push a small piece of dried spaghetti through the centre of the upper body. Brush the base of the upper body with a little edible glue, then attach it to the skirt, pushing the

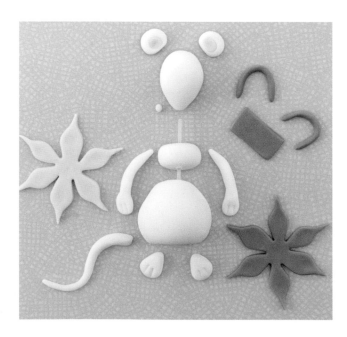

spaghetti through the centre of the skirt as you do so **(b)** – this will support the upper body and head. Trim the dried spaghetti, if necessary.

6 For the arms, roll 2 pea-sized balls of white modelling paste into thin sausages and lightly pinch them in at the wrists. Flatten the hands slightly and indent a couple of lines with the sharp knife for fingers. Attach the arms to the top of the body with edible glue **(c)**.

7 For the dress straps, roll a pea-sized ball of purple modelling paste into a very thin sausage and cut it into 2 lengths, each about 3cm/1¼in. For the front of the dress, roll out the remaining purple modelling paste quite thinly and cut a rectangle about 2.5cm x 1cm/1 x ½in. Using edible glue, attach the straps to the upper body, followed by the front of the dress.

8 Brush the base of the head with edible glue and attach to the upper body, inserting the centre of the head onto the dried spaghetti **(d)**.

9 To make the ears, roll a little white modelling paste into 2 pea-sized balls and indent the centre of each one with the small head of the ball tool or with the tip of your little finger. For the pink centres, roll 2 tiny balls of pale pink modelling paste and flatten them slightly. Attach the pink centres to the ears, then attach the ears to the head, securing both with edible glue. For the nose, roll a tiny ball of

(a)   **(b)**

(c)   **(d)**

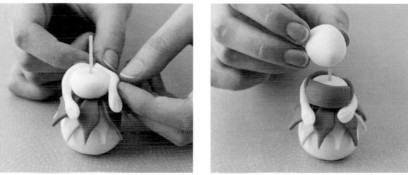

pale pink modelling paste and attach it to the head with edible glue. For the eyes, put a little black food paste colouring in a small bowl. Dilute with 1–2 drops of water, then carefully paint the eyes onto the mouse's face **(e)**.

10 For the tail, roll a large pea-sized ball of white modelling paste into a thin, tapering sausage, and mould the tail as you would like it to look on the finished cake. Do not attach the tail to the mouse. Place the tail on a flat surface and leave it to dry overnight, uncovered, in a cool, dry place.

11 To make the daisy stalks, roll out the dark green modelling paste into a long, very thin sausage and cut it into 8 lengths, each about 2.5cm/1in long. Attach 1 stalk to one of the mouse's hands with a little edible glue. Place the remaining daisy stalks on a flat surface, curving each one slightly as you do so. Leave the daisy stalks to dry overnight, uncovered, in a cool, dry place.

12 Roll out the remaining white modelling paste quite thinly and stamp out at least 8 daisies using the daisy plunger cutter. Roll out at least 8 tiny balls of the pale yellow modelling paste and attach each one to the centre of a daisy with a little edible glue. Place the daisies on the indented foam pad – this will help them take on a slightly curved shape when they dry. Leave the daisies, mouse and sugar paste covered cake to dry overnight, uncovered, in a cool, dry place.

13 When all the elements have dried, assemble the cake. Place the mouse's feet on top of the cake, securing them in place with a little edible glue. Brush the flattened sides of the feet and the base of the mouse's body with edible glue and carefully rest the body on top of the feet. Position the tail and attach with a little edible glue **(f)**. Attach one of the daisies to the end of the stalk in the mouse's hand **(g)**. Arrange the rest of the stalks and daisies on top of the cake and falling down the side to create a daisy chain, securing with edible glue. Wrap the ribbon around the base of the cake, securing the join at the back with a little edible glue and trimming as necessary. Leave to dry completely.

(e)

(f)

(g)

CHAPTER FIVE

It's time to reveal my best-kept secrets! Baking and decorating can take a lot of preparation, but with a little know-how you'll be able to make delicious decorated treats with ease. From tools and equipment to techniques and templates, you'll find everything you need and more in this chapter to create beautiful baked goodies time and time again.

BEST-KEPT
SECRETS

Basic Equipment

The following basic items will all be very useful when you are making, baking and icing the cakes and biscuits in this book. Items needed for specific projects are listed on the recipe pages. You'll probably find that you already own a lot of the equipment listed in the baking section. Biscuit cutters used in specific recipes can be replaced by templates, especially if you only have to cut out a small number of shapes (see pages 162–171). For larger quantities however, I do recommend purchasing cutters. They are inexpensive and widely available.

The equipment listed in the icing and decorating sections is extremely useful, especially if you intend to make lots of cakes and biscuits. The cake leveller, for instance, is a particularly handy tool that will allow you to level and split your sponge cakes quickly and easily, but a long serrated knife can always be used instead. Other items like plunger cutters will make your life much easier when trying to create large quantities of small sugar paste decorations – a task that could feel insurmountable if attempted by hand.

Now that so many of us are starting to be more creative with our cake making, you'll find that all of the equipment listed is readily available. I have listed a few of my favourite suppliers on page 172.

BAKING EQUIPMENT

Baking parchment

(1) Baking sheets

Baking tins

(2) Ball tins

(3) Biscuit cutters

(4) Cake tins (in a range of different shapes and sizes)

(5) Ceramic baking beans

(6) Circle cutters (1–8cm/½–3¼in in diameter)

(7) Cooling racks

(8) Cupcake cases

Electric mixers – a freestanding or hand-held electric mixer with beater and whisk attachments will make preparing your cake mixture and biscuit dough much easier.

Kitchen scales – ideally digital for accuracy.

(9) Mixing bowls/Heatproof bowls

(10) Muffin tins (12-cup and 24-cup)

(11) Palette knife (large) –used to transfer hot, just-baked biscuits onto cooling racks.

(12) Rolling pin (large)

(13) Sieve

(14) Spatula – used for mixing and spreading. Spatulas with a broad, flexible plastic or silicone blade are ideal for these jobs.

Spring-action-release ice cream scoop – used to measure out whoopie pie mixture before baking. Scoops are a brilliant way to ensure you end up with an even batch.

(15) Wooden spoon

ICING EQUIPMENT

(1) Cake cards (also known as boards) – make it easier to move cakes into position on plates or cake stands and are particularly handy for mini cakes. They are slightly thinner than cake drums but can also be used to stabilize tiered cakes.

(2) Cake drums – used to stabilize tiered cakes and ensure that the plastic dowels do not penetrate the layer above. They make any cake easy to transport. Normally silver in colour, they can also be covered in sugar paste and used as a decorative base to complement your finished cake. For an elegant finish, use the same colour of sugar paste to cover the drum that you used to cover the cake. For a dramatic finish, use a contrasting colour.

(3) Cake leveller – used to level and split sponge cakes (not suitable for use on fruit cakes). It has a variable height adjustment, so you can cut your layers to the desired depth.

Cake turntable – used when decorating the side(s) of a cake. Tilting turntables are ideal for this job.

(4) Dipping forks – used for dipping chocolates and truffles in melted coatings; 2- or 3-pronged dipping forks are also extremely helpful when dipping fancies in fondant icing.

Dowelling guide – used to mark the position of the dowels to be inserted into the tiers of a stacked cake (see page 171).

(5) Dowels – used to support cake tiers from collapsing into the tier below and should be used in conjunction with a cake drum. Dowels are usually made of plastic and should be cut to the correct length with a strong pair of scissors or clippers.

(6) Icing nozzles – used for piping frosting onto cupcakes and to pipe fillings onto macarons and whoopie pies. I usually use 14mm/⅝in closed-star, open-star and plain nozzles.

(7) Icing smoothers – used to achieve a smooth, flat surface after covering cakes with sugar paste or marzipan. They will help you to achieve a perfect, professional finish.

(8) Marzipan spacers – are used when rolling out sugar paste, marzipan or biscuit dough to give you an even thickness. I usually use 5mm/¼in spacers.

(9) Metal side scraper – used to achieve a smooth, even finish after covering the side(s) of a cake in buttercream or chocolate ganache.

(10) Offset palette knives – a large offset palette knife is used to add fillings to cakes and to assist you when stacking cake tiers. A small offset palette knife is used to lift small amounts of sugar paste onto biscuits to prevent the sugar paste from stretching.

(11) Paper lollipop sticks – inserted into cake pops or the base of cupcakes. They can also be used to push into uncooked biscuit dough prior to cooking, to create biscuits on sticks.

(12) Pastry brush – used to brush sugar syrup over sponge cakes.

(13) Piping bags – used for piping large amounts of buttercream, frosting or meringue. Large disposable or heavy-duty synthetic piping bags are ideal for this job.

(14) Rolling pin (small) – used for rolling out sugar, flower and modelling pastes.

(15) Ruler – used for measuring rolled-out sugar paste when specific sizes need to be cut. Metal rulers are ideal for this job.

(16) Sharp knife – used to achieve a clean finish when cutting out marzipan, biscuit dough and sugar, flower and modelling pastes.

Spirit level (small) – used when levelling and layering cakes. Ensuring your cake has a level top early on in the process means that it is less likely to tilt during the stacking process. Not to be shared with the tool box!

(17) Spring-action-release ice cream scoop – used to measure out truffle mixture to ensure you end up with an even batch.

(18) Squeeze icing bottles – used for squeezing flood-consistency royal icing over the surface of outlined biscuits. A brilliant piece of equipment for the biscuit projects in this book.

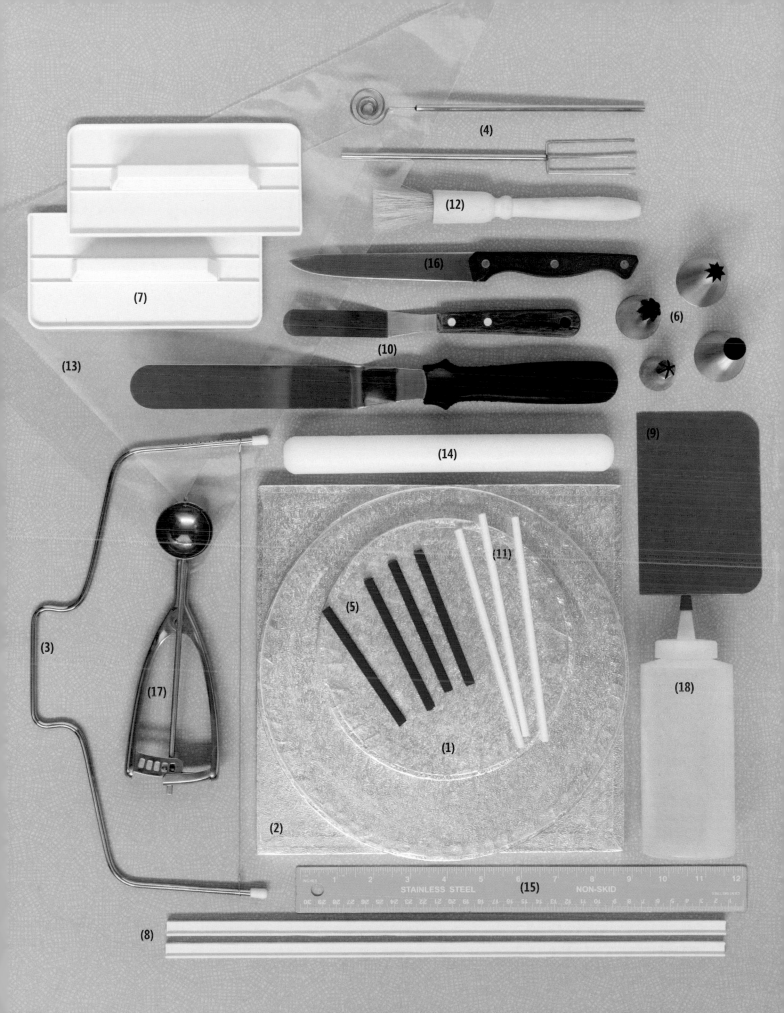

DECORATING EQUIPMENT

Tools

(1) Ball tool (double-headed) – an essential tool, used to shape the petals of sugar flowers, for round indentations and for adding detail to sugar paste decorations.

(2) Craft knife – a small, sharp-bladed knife used when working with sugar paste sheets or chocolate transfers, or for intricate sugarcraft work.

(3) Design wheeler tool – a detailing tool used to create pattern designs on sugar, flower and modelling pastes. It has three interchangeable design heads: fluted, stitch and rounded wheel. The stitch head is used on several of the projects in this book.

(4) Foam pad – a flat, springy surface used in conjunction with a ball tool (see above) to give sugar paste flowers a more natural look.

(5) Hydrangea cutter and veining mould set – consisting of a steel flower cutter and a veiner mould, this invaluable set will help you create realistic hydrangea flowers with ease.

(6) Icing nozzles – the no. 2 and the no. 1.5 plain icing nozzles are used for piping royal icing onto biscuits or to add intricate details onto cakes and biscuits.

(7) Indented foam pad (also known as a profile sheet) – a curvy, springy surface on which to place sugar paste flowers or leaves when leaving them to dry overnight. It allows the edges of your leaves and flowers to dry with a slight curved shape to give sugarcraft creations a more natural form.

(8) Leaf veiner mat – used to give sugar paste leaves a more natural look, by lightly rolling the mat over the top of the leaf.

(9) Moulds – a selection of delicate silicone moulds used to create detailed sugar and modelling paste decorations for cakes, cupcakes or biscuits. Sugarcraft moulds come in a vast array of shapes and designs. Sugar or modelling paste is pushed into the mould, then the moulded paste is turned out and left to dry.

(10) Paintbrushes – used when handpainting intricate details onto cakes and sugar or modelling paste models, and for brushing edible glue onto cakes and biscuits and sugarcraft decorations.

Piping bags – used to pipe royal icing details onto cakes and biscuits. Small disposable or homemade piping bags are ideal.

(11) Plunger cutters – either plain or embossed, these tools create quick and easy shapes from rolled-out sugar or flower paste.

(12) Scriber – used to indent patterns or dots or to transfer a design onto sugar paste. It is also useful for popping any air bubbles that may appear in the sugar paste, particularly when covering cakes.

(13) Stencils – culinary stencils made from food-grade plastic. Used with royal icing or edible dusts or powders, they are an extremely effective way to add patterns to cakes and biscuits.

(14) Straight frill cutters – used to stamp out a range of basic border designs from rolled out sugar or modelling paste.

(15) Sugar paste cutters – made of either steel or plastic and available in a huge range of flower and leaf shapes. For use with rolled-out sugar, modelling or flower pastes.

(16) Veiner tool – used to create a vein pattern on sugarcraft flowers or leaves.

Edible Decorations

(17) Dragees – edible sugar balls used to add a decorative, edible element to your cake or biscuits. Available in various colours.

Edible colours – edible pastes and dusts come in a huge range of colours. Pastes can be used to colour fondant, sugar, flower and modelling pastes, buttercream, royal icing and marzipan. Dusts are used to add colour accents to dried sugarcraft decorations.

(18) Edible glitter/lustre dusts – non-toxic glitters can be used to add sparkle to your creations. Lustre dusts can be brushed on dry to sugar-paste decorations to create a shimmering glow, or can be mixed with water to make an edible paint.

(19) Pen with edible ink – useful for adding small details to sugar paste models if you don't have any edible paint. They are also ideal for marking the position of dowels when stacking cakes.

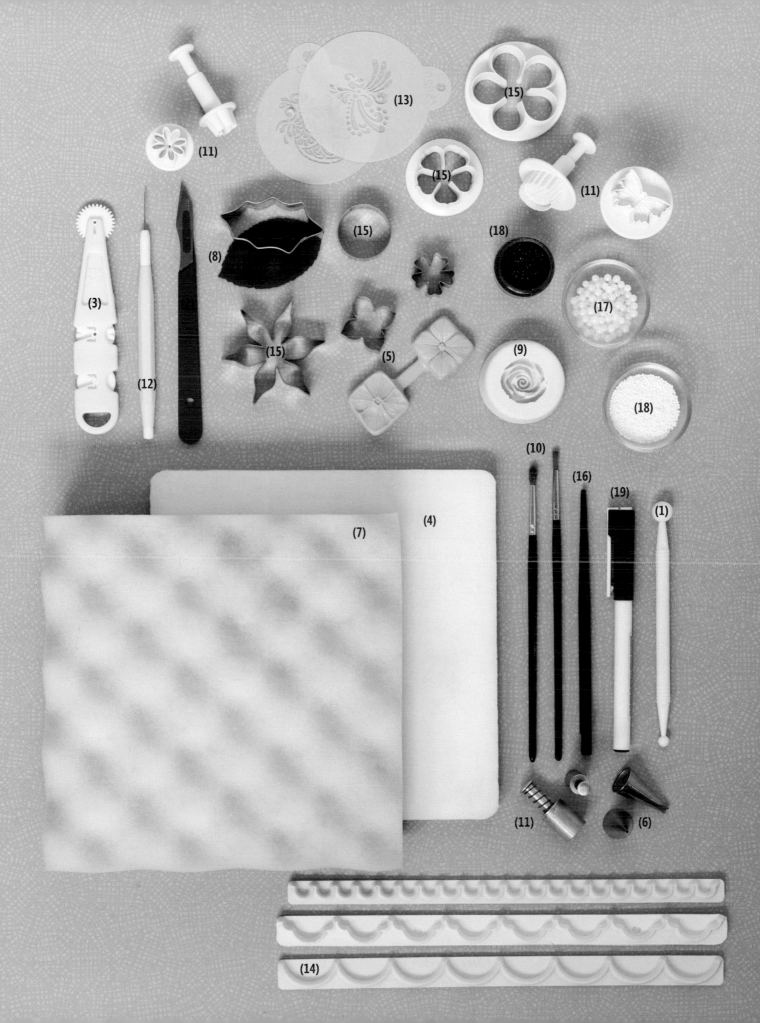

Preparing Biscuits for Baking

1 recipe quantity Biscuit Dough
   of your choice (see pages
   26–7)

YOU WILL NEED
baking parchment
2 baking sheets
rolling pin
5mm/¼in marzipan spacers
   (optional)
biscuit template or biscuit cutter
sharp knife
large palette knife

TIPS
If you want to make your own template, draw your own design on card and cut out the template, then cut round this on the dough. Alternatively, use a biscuit cutter.

If the dough has been out of the fridge for a long time during the cutting-out process, put it back in the fridge and leave it to firm up for a while before baking.

1 Roll the dough into a ball, then divide it in half. Tightly wrap half of the dough in cling film and chill in the fridge until needed. Cut 4 sheets of baking parchment slightly larger than a baking sheet. Lay one of the sheets of baking parchment on the work surface, then place the remaining dough in the centre of the sheet **(a)**.

2 Lay another sheet of baking parchment over the top of the dough, then, using the rolling pin, roll out the dough until it is about 5mm/¼in thick, using marzipan spacers if you like **(b)**. Slide the dough, within the sheets of baking parchment, onto one of the baking sheets. Remove the chilled ball of dough from the fridge and repeat as above, then stack the baking sheets on top of each other and chill in the fridge for at least 2 hours or overnight to allow the dough to firm up before cutting. If the dough is soft during the cutting-out process, the biscuits will not hold their shape well.

3 When the dough is firm, remove one of the baking sheets from the fridge and slide the dough, within the sheets of baking parchment, onto the work surface. Reline the baking sheet with baking parchment and leave to one side. Gently remove the top sheet of baking parchment from the dough and reserve until needed.

4 Place a biscuit template on top of the rolled dough and cut around it as often as required **(c)**, leaving as little space as possible between the shapes. Roll the trimmings into a ball, then lay the reserved sheet of baking parchment over the top. Re-roll the dough and cut out more biscuits as above until all the dough has been used up.

5 Using the palette knife, transfer the biscuits to the lined baking sheet, spacing them 3cm/1¼in apart to allow each one to spread slightly during cooking. Chill the cut-out biscuits in the fridge while you repeat steps 3 and 4 with the remaining rolled dough.

(a)

(b)

(c)

Lining Cake Tins

butter, softened, for greasing

YOU WILL NEED
cake tin
baking parchment
pen with edible ink or a pencil
scissors
ruler

LINING ROUND AND HEART-SHAPED TINS

1 For the base of the tin, place your cake tin on a sheet of baking parchment and draw around it with the edible pen. Cut out the shape along the inside of the line so that the circle or heart shape fits neatly into the bottom of the tin, then leave to one side until needed.

2 For the side of the tin, cut out a strip of baking parchment that is long enough to line the side of the tin with a small overlap, and that is at least 5cm/2in higher than the side of the tin. Fold up one of the long edges of the strip by 2.5cm/1in and make a firm crease. Open out the fold, then cut little vertical slits all the way along the folded edge up to the crease, creating a frilled strip.

3 Grease the inside of the cake tin with butter, then gently press the frilled strip of baking parchment into the tin, allowing the frilled-edge to sit on the base of the tin. Place the circle or heart piece of baking parchment in the bottom of the tin, covering the frilled strip.

LINING SQUARE TINS

Follow steps 1 and 2 as above. Grease the inside of the cake tin with butter, then gently press the frilled strip of baking parchment into the tin, allowing the frilled edge to sit on the base of the tin. Overlap the frills in each corner to allow the baking parchment to fit neatly into the corners of the tin, then run your finger up and down the corner edges to create 4 sharp creases – this will ensure the cake will have sharp corners when you remove it from the tin. Place the square piece of baking parchment in the bottom of the tin, covering the frilled strip.

LINING BALL CAKE TINS

1 Cut out a circle of baking parchment with a diameter about 5cm/2in wider than the diameter of the cups that form the ball tin. Cut 3 slits halfway towards the centre of the circle, evenly spacing them around the side.

2 Grease one of the cups in the ball tin with butter, then place the circle of baking parchment into the cup. Repeat as necessary.

Layering & Filling Cakes

FOR SPONGE, RICH
CHOCOLATE OR
MARBLE CAKES
1 or 2 Rich Chocolate, Sponge or
   Marble Cakes (see pages 56–7,
   62–3 or 76–7)
Buttercream and/or seedless
   raspberry jam or Chocolate
   Ganache (see page 16)
Sugar Syrup (see page 119)

YOU WILL NEED
cake leveller or long serrated
   knife and a ruler
baking parchment
cake drum or cake card
offset palette knife
pastry brush

TIPS
For a deep layered sponge, bake
two cakes and sandwich all four
layers together.

Ideally, make the cake(s) the day
before you need to layer and
fill to prevent the cake(s) from
crumbling when cut. If time is
short, chill the cake(s) in the
fridge for at least 2 hours before
levelling and layering them.

Whenever you need to layer and fill a sponge, rich chocolate or marble cake, simply follow the method below using the quantity of sugar syrup and fillings specified by a particular recipe or by the charts on page 155 to achieve perfect results.

1 Using the cake leveller, level the top of the cake(s) **(a)**, then cut the cake(s) in half horizontally **(b)**. Alternatively, use a serrated knife and a ruler to level and cut the cake(s) in half.

2 Cut a piece of baking parchment slightly larger than the cake drum. Lay the piece of baking parchment on the work surface and place the cake drum on top – this will make the cake easier to turn when filling. Spread a very thin layer of buttercream over the top of the cake drum, then carefully place the first layer of cake over the top – the buttercream will anchor the cake to the drum.

3 If layering and filling one cake, lightly brush the top of the first layer with sugar syrup, then spread a thin layer of buttercream over the top with the offset palette knife, followed by a thin layer of jam, if using, over the top. Carefully place the second layer of the cake on top of the first, then gently press the layers together with your hands to secure the sandwich.

If layering and filling two cakes, lightly brush the top of the first layer with sugar syrup, then spread a thin layer of buttercream over the top with the offset palette knife. Carefully place the second layer of cake on top of the first. Lightly brush the top of the second layer with sugar syrup and spread a thin layer of buttercream, or jam if preferred, over the top **(c)**. Carefully place the third layer of the cake on top of the second, then lightly brush with sugar syrup and spread a thin layer of buttercream over the top. Carefully place the fourth layer on top, then gently press the layers together with your hands to secure the sandwich.

(a)

(b)

(c)

Covering Fancies in Fondant Icing

FOR FONDANT FANCIES
marizpan-topped fancies
   (see page 18)
freshly made fondant icing
   (see page 18)

YOU WILL NEED
wire cooling rack
baking parchment
dipping fork or table fork
foil or paper cupcake cases

TIP
When arranging the fancies in a tight square, ensure the sides of the cakes are touching – this will help the cases to hold their square shape while the icing dries.

Whenever you need to cover fancies in fondant icing, simply follow the method below using the quantity of prepared fancies and fondant icing specified by the recipe.

1 Place a wire cooling rack over a sheet of baking parchment and remove the marzipan-topped fancies from the fridge. Covering one cake at a time, carefully dip one of the fancies marzipan-side down into the fondant icing until the fondant covers about three-quarters of each side **(a)**. Using a dipping fork, carefully lift the fancy out of the fondant, allowing any excess icing to fall back into the bowl **(b)**, then immediately transfer the dipped fancy to the prepared cooling rack and leave to dry for 10 minutes. Repeat with the remaining fancies and fondant icing. Store any unused fondant icing in an airtight container until needed.

2 After 10 minutes, carefully place each fancy into a cupcake case **(c)**, then mould the round case around the square cake, pinching the case into 4 corners as you do so **(d)**. Arrange the fancies in a tight square and leave to dry until the icing has completely set.

(a)

(b)

(c)

(d)

Covering Cakes with Buttercream or Chocolate Ganache

Whenever you need to cover a cake or cupcake in buttercream or chocolate ganache, simply follow the method below using the quantity of buttercream or ganache specified by a particular recipe or by the chart on page 155 to achieve perfect results.

FOR CAKES

FOR 1 CAKE
1 or 2 layered and filled cake(s)
 (see page 150)
Buttercream or Chocolate
 Ganache (see page 16)

YOU WILL NEED
baking parchment
large offset palette knife
metal side scraper

1 Cut a piece of baking parchment slightly larger than the cake drum or base of the cake. Lay the piece of baking parchment on the work surface and place the cake on top – this will make the cake easier to turn when covering. Using the offset palette knife, cover the side of the cake with buttercream or ganache **(a)**, working smoothly and neatly until the side is completely covered in a thin, even layer. Make sure the covering on the side of the cake is smooth and even by gently running the side scraper along the side of the cake **(b)**, slowly turning the cake as you do so.

2 Holding the offset palette knife at a slight angle, spread a thin, even layer of buttercream or ganache over the top of the cake, taking care to keep the top edge neat. Make sure the covering on top of the cake is smooth and even by gently running the side scraper over the top.

FOR CUPCAKES

FOR 1 CUPCAKE
Buttercream or Chocolate
 Ganache (see page 16)
cupcake (see page 129), baked
 in a paper or foil cupcake case

YOU WILL NEED
small offset palette knife

Put a little buttercream or ganache on the tip of the offset palette knife and spread it onto the centre of a cupcake. Spread the topping over the top of the cupcake, pushing it towards the edges of the case and adding more buttercream or ganache as necessary. For a textured finish, spread the topping over the cake in circular motions with the flat tip of the offset palette knife, indenting the topping slightly as you do so to create subtle peaks **(c)**. For a smooth finish, spread the topping over the cake in circular motions with the flat tip of the offset palette knife, taking care not to indent the topping.

(a)

(b)

(c)

Covering Cakes with Sugar Paste and Marzipan

Whenever you need to cover a cake with sugar paste (or with marzipan and sugar paste), simply follow the method below using the quantities specified by a particular recipe or by the chart on page 155. If you are new to covering cakes, start with slightly more sugar paste or marzipan than specified so you have plenty to work with.

FOR 1 CAKE
icing sugar, for dusting
sugar paste
1 covered Rich Chocolate, Sponge, Marble or Fruit Cake (see pages 56–7, 62–3, 76–7)

YOU WILL NEED
rolling pin
5mm/¼in marzipan spacers (optional)
2 icing smoothers
sharp knife
scriber or sharp needle

IN ADDITION TO THE ABOVE
apricot jam, warmed or buttercream
marzipan

YOU WILL NEED
pastry brush or offset palette knife

COVERING CAKES WITH SUGAR PASTE

Dust the work surface with a little icing sugar, then knead the sugar paste until it is soft and pliable. Roll out the kneaded sugar paste until it is 5mm/¼in thick, using marzipan spacers if you like. Carefully lift the rolled sugar paste and gently place it over the top and side(s) of the cake, taking care not to stretch or pull it. Use your hands to smooth it over the top and side(s) of the cake, making sure to smooth out any air bubbles **(a)**. For a flat, smooth finish, smooth the top and side(s) of the cake again with icing smoothers **(b)**. Trim off any excess sugar paste at the base of the cake with the sharp knife **(c)**. Use the scriber to prick out any remaining air bubbles in the sugar paste.

COVERING CAKES WITH MARZIPAN AND SUGAR PASTE

If covering a fruit cake, lightly brush the top and side(s) of the cake with a thin layer of apricot jam using a pastry brush. If using a sponge cake, lightly cover the top and side(s) of the cake with a thick layer of buttercream using the offset palette knife. Dust the work surface with a little icing sugar, then knead the marzipan until it has just softened – take care not to over-knead the marzipan as this will make it oily. Roll out the kneaded marzipan until it is 5mm/¼in thick, using marzipan spacers if you like, and cover the cake as above. Leave the cake overnight, uncovered, in a cool, dry place to allow the marzipan to set. When the marzipan has set, brush the top and side(s) of the cake with a little cooled, boiled water, then roll out the sugar paste as above and cover the cake.

(a)

(b)

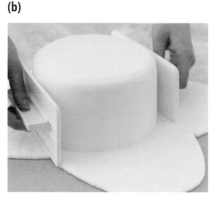

(c)

Covering Cake Drums with Sugar Paste

FOR 1 DRUM
icing sugar, for dusting
sugar paste

YOU WILL NEED
pastry brush
cake drum
rolling pin
5mm/¼in marzipan spacers (optional)
icing smoother
sharp knife
scriber or sharp needle
length of ribbon long enough to fit around the edge of the drum, about 1.5cm/⅝in wide
double-sided tape or a glue stick

Whenever you need to cover a cake drum in sugar paste, simply follow the method below using the quantities specified by a particular recipe or by using the chart opposite. If you are new to covering cakes, start with slightly more sugar paste than specified so you have plenty of sugar paste to work with.

1 Using the pastry brush, lightly brush the top of the cake drum with cold water **(a)**. Dust the work surface with a little icing sugar, then knead the sugar paste until it is soft and pliable. Roll out the sugar paste until it is 5mm/¼in thick, using marzipan spacers if you like **(b)**.

2 Carefully lift the rolled sugar paste and gently place it over the top of the cake drum **(c)**, taking care not to stretch or pull it. Use your hands to smooth it over the top of the drum, making sure to smooth out any air bubbles. For a flat, smooth finish, smooth the top of the sugar paste again with the icing smoother **(d)**. Trim off any excess sugar paste with the sharp knife **(e).** Use the scriber to prick out any remaining air bubbles in the sugar paste.

3 Wrap the ribbon around the side of the cake drum **(f)**, securing the join at the back with double-sided tape and trimming as necessary.

(a) **(b)** **(c)**

(d) **(e)** **(f)**

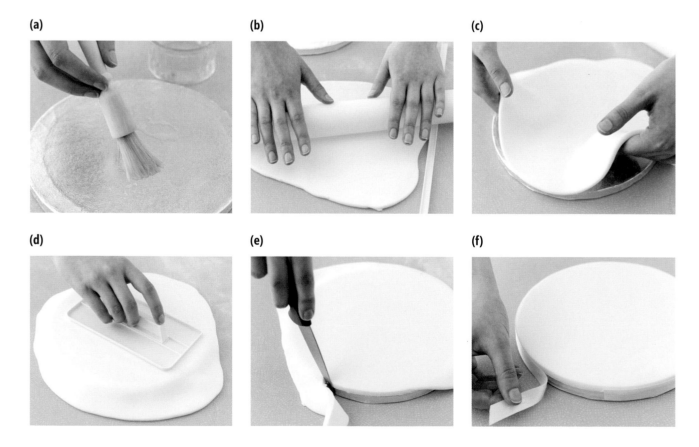

Covering Cakes and Cake Drums

Whenever you need to cover a cake drum in sugar paste; cover a cake in sugar paste or marzipan; or cover a cake or cupcake with buttercream or chocolate ganache, simply follow the methods on pages 152–154 and use the quantity of sugar paste, marzipan or buttercream or ganache specified by the charts below.

Sugar paste quantities for covering cake drums	
Cake drum	Sugar paste
10cm/4in	170g/6oz
13cm/5in	200g/7oz
15cm/6in	300g/10½oz
18cm/7in	400g/14oz
20cm/8in	550g/1lb 4oz
23cm/9in	700g/1lb 8oz
25cm/10in	750g/1lb 10oz

Sugar paste/marzipan quantities for covering cakes	
Cake	Sugar paste/ marzipan
10cm/4in	400g/14oz
13cm/5in	500g/1lb 2oz
15cm/6in	600g/1lb 5oz
18cm/7in	750g/1lb 10oz
20cm/8in	850g/1lb 14oz
23cm/9in	1kg/2lb 4oz
25cm/10in	1.25kg/2lb 12oz

Buttercream and chocolate ganache quantities for covering cakes and cupcakes	
Cake	Buttercream/ chocolate ganache
10cm/4in	175g/6oz
13cm/5in	250g/9oz
15cm/6in	300g/10½oz
18cm/7in	450g/1lb
20cm/8in	500g/1lb 2oz
23cm/9in	750g/1lb 10oz
25cm/10in	1kg/2lb 4oz
12 cupcakes/24 mini cupcakes	350g/12oz

Stacking Tiered Cakes

2 or more cake tiers of different sizes, covered with sugar paste and attached to cake drums or boards the same size as the cakes
stiff-peak Royal Icing (see page 46)

YOU WILL NEED
dowelling guide
  (see page 171)
scriber or sharp needle
plastic dowels (4 for each tier
  except the top one)
pen with edible ink
strong scissors or clippers
small offset palette knife
large offset palette knife
2 icing smoothers
spirit level (optional)

TIPS
Cakes covered in sugar paste should be allowed to dry overnight, uncovered, in a cool, dry place before they are stacked.

If the dowels are hollow, cut them to size with strong scissors. If the dowels are solid, you will need strong clippers. Alternatively, score the dowels with a sharp knife, then snap them to achieve the correct height.

1 Place the bottom tier on the work surface and position the dowelling guide over the top of the cake. Using the dowelling guide, select the position of the dowels according to the size of the following tier, then mark the position of the first four dowels by lightly pricking the top of the cake with the scriber **(a)**. When selecting the position of the dowels, bear in mind that they need to be placed inside the diameter of the following tier to hide them from view.

2 Push the dowels straight down into the cake until they are resting on the cake drum **(b)**. Using the pen with edible ink, mark each dowel at the point at which it protrudes from the top of the cake – the mark should be level with the top of the cake. Remove the marked dowels from the cake then line them up on the work surface and assess the average height of the marked lines. Using the strong scissors, cut down each dowel to the average height, then push them back into the cake.

3 Using the small offset palette knife, spread a small amount of royal icing in a thin layer over the area between the dowels **(c)** – the royal icing will anchor the following tier in place. Using the large offset palette knife to help you, carefully place the following tier on top of the dowels **(d)**. Move the tier into the centre with icing smoothers. Check that the top tier is level, using a spirit level if you like, then leave the cake for 10 minutes or so to allow the icing to set. Repeat for further tiers as necessary.

(a)　　　　　　　　　　　　　　**(b)**

(c)　　　　　　　　　　　　　　**(d)**

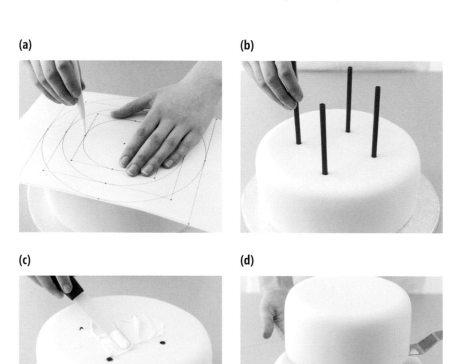

Piping Tips and Techniques

PREPARING TO PIPE

stiff- or soft-peak Royal Icing
  (see page 46) or Frosting
  (see page 118)

YOU WILL NEED
nozzle (optional)
piping bag

TIP
If the nozzle does not sit
comfortably at the tip of the bag
the icing will be pushed out of the
gap between the nozzle and the
bag and you will not be able to
pipe effectively.

1 Select a nozzle and insert it into the piping bag. If you are using a disposable piping bag, snip off the tip before inserting the nozzle. To fit a small nozzle, gradually snip off the tip of the piping bag until about half of the nozzle sits comfortably into the tip of the bag. To fit a large nozzle, gradually snip off the tip of the piping bag until the end of the nozzle sits comfortably into the tip of the bag.

2 Fill the piping bag with icing or frosting, taking care never to fill it more than about one-third full. Using the back of your hand, ease the filling towards the nozzle, expelling any air in the bag as you do so. Fold the top corners of the bag towards the centre to stop the icing from escaping. Fold the top of the bag towards the tip, then fold again to secure. Hold the bag in your dominant hand, then lightly place two fingers from your non-dominant hand near the base of the nozzle to steady the bag.

PIPING FROSTING SWIRLS

Frosting (see page 118)

YOU WILL NEED
large plain, open-star or closed-
  star (not shown) nozzle
large heavy-duty piping bag

Select a nozzle and insert it into the piping bag, then prepare to pipe as above.

High Swirls add extra height to cupcakes. They are often used to decorate cupcakes and feature in most of the cupcake recipes in this book. To pipe a high swirl, hold the piping bag vertically, then, starting at the edge of the cupcake, pipe the frosting in a fluid spiral motion towards the centre, slightly overlapping the frosting as you work – this will give the swirl height.

Flat Swirls produce a lovely rose-like effect, as you'll find in the Rose Swirl Cupcakes recipe (see page 22). To pipe a flat swirl, hold the bag vertically, then starting at the centre of the cupcake, pipe the frosting in a fluid spiral motion towards the edge, taking care not to overlap the frosting.

**High Swirl, piped with
a large plain nozzle**

**High Swirl, piped with
a large open-star nozzle**

**Flat Swirl, piped with a
large open-star nozzle**

MAKING A DISPOSABLE PIPING BAG

Disposable piping bags are readily available and come in a variety of sizes, but it's also easy to make your own out of baking parchment.

YOU WILL NEED
baking parchment
ruler
scissors

TIP
Homemade piping bags are great for piping royal icing, but piping intricate details requires a nozzle for this level of decoration so shop-bought bags are best.

1 Cut a 30 x 30cm/12 x 12in square of baking parchment. Fold the square in half diagonally and make a firm crease. Cut along the crease to make two triangles in total.

2 Take one of the parchment triangles, and place it on the work surface with the longest side furthest away from you. Take the top left-hand point in your right hand and curl it under until it touches the bottom point – the parchment should form a cone during this process **(a)**. Hold the two points firmly together in your left hand **(b)**. With your right hand, curl the top right-hand point **(c)** over the top of the existing cone until all the points meet and a definite cone shape has formed.

3 Holding the points between you thumb and forefingers, gently shuffle the position of the points until you form a very sharp point at the tip of the cone.

4 Fold the triangle formed at the base of the cone towards the tip, then fold again to secure **(d)**. The bag is now ready to be filled with stiff- or soft-peak royal icing. Snip off the tip before use.

(a) **(b)**

(c) **(d)**

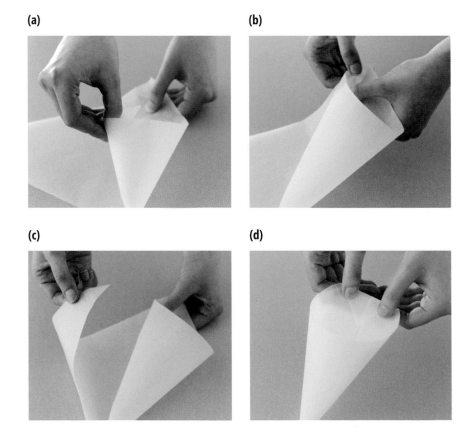

PIPING ROYAL ICING

Due to its incredibly versatile nature, royal icing is used for a range of decorating techniques, from icing biscuits and piping intricate details to securing sugar paste decorations and building gingerbread houses. Depending on its purpose, it is made up to one of three consistencies: stiff-peak, soft-peak and flood-consistency (see page 46). Stiff- and soft-peak consistencies should be spooned into a piping bag before use. (Flood-consistency royal icing should be transferred to a squeeze icing bottle before using.)

Select a small nozzle and insert it into a piping bag, or simply snip the tip off the end of a disposable bag.

Piping Intricate Dots, Teardrops and Lines

soft-peak Royal Icing (see page 46)

YOU WILL NEED
piping bag, fitted with a small nozzle
small paintbrush (optional)

TIP
If you are decorating a cake, you may find it easier placing the cake on a tilting turntable, tilting away from you when piping details onto the side(s) of the cake.

Following the instructions on page 157, fill a piping bag with soft-peak royal icing and prepare to pipe.

Dots – hold the piping bag at a right angle to the surface of your cake or biscuit. Holding the nozzle about 1mm/$\frac{1}{16}$in away from the surface, gently squeeze a small amount of icing out of the bag to form a dot, then carefully lift the nozzle away. The more you squeeze the bag, the bigger the dot will be. If a peak forms on top of the dot, flatten it with a small, dampened paintbrush.

Teardrops – create a dot as above, then drag the nozzle through the top of the dot to create a teardrop shape.

Lines – with the tip of the nozzle touching the surface of your cake or biscuit, gently squeeze the icing out the bag, then lift the bag slightly away from the surface and pipe a line, applying a slow, even pressure to the bag as you do so. To end the line, bring the tip of the nozzle back to the surface, then gently pull it away.

Stiff-Peak Royal Icing

Soft-Peak Royal Icing

Flood-Consistency Royal Icing

Sugar Paste, Flower Paste and Modelling Paste

These three forms of fondant icing can be used in many different ways to decorate cakes and biscuits. Of the three types, sugar paste is the most widely available and most commonly used, but all three can be bought at specialist cake shops and online, though I prefer to make my own modelling paste.

SUGAR PASTE

This sweet fondant icing is used as a final covering for cakes and cake drums and can also be formed into simple decorations such as plain leaves and flowers. It's widely available and easy to use – it's pliable, rolls out well and dries with a lovely smooth (slightly shiny) surface.

FLOWER PASTE

Flower paste (also known as "petal paste"), is a more pliable form of sugar paste. You can roll it out more thinly than sugar paste without risk of it tearing and it also dries much harder. It's readily available from specialist suppliers (see page 172) and is mainly used in much smaller quantities for detailed decorations that require delicate moulding such as the roses for the Rose Cupcakes (see page 126) and the Magnificent Mini Cakes (see page 121), and the ribbon detail for the Orange Pomander Cake (see page 94).

MODELLING PASTE

Adding sodium carboxymethylcellulose (CMC) to sugar paste creates an icing known as modelling paste which is stronger than sugar paste. Modelling paste takes longer to dry than sugar paste, but it also dries much harder, making it good for cakes requiring larger icing decorations, such as the corsages for the Ivory Corsage Wedding Cake on page 114, the teddy bears and rabbits for the Baby Shower Cupcakes on page 110 and the handle and spout for the Teapot Cake on page 122.

Making Modelling Paste

To make modelling paste, sprinkle 1 teaspoon of CMC straight onto the work surface and then knead 350g/12oz sugar paste into it and transfer to an airtight container. The sugar paste will start to thicken immediately, and will continue to do so over a period of 24 hours.

Using Sugar Paste, Flower Paste and Modelling Paste

• Before rolling or moulding sugar, flower or modelling paste, dust the work surface with a little icing sugar. Knead sugar and modelling pastes until they are soft and pliable. Knead flower paste until it is smooth and elastic, pulling it apart to soften it if necessary.

• White sugar, flower or modelling paste can be coloured with food colouring pastes. To colour, simply spread a small amount of food colouring paste onto the sugar, flower or modelling paste using the end of a cocktail stick, and knead until combined. Repeat until the desired colour is achieved.

• Once exposed to the air, sugar, flower and modelling pastes will gradually harden. If you are working in batches or delicately moulding a small amount of paste, take care to store the remaining paste in an airtight container until needed to prevent it from drying out and cracking.

Rolling out Sugar Paste, Flower Paste and Modelling Paste

• When a recipe states to roll out sugar, flower or modelling paste "very thinly", roll out the kneaded paste until it is about 1–2mm/$\frac{1}{16}$in thick.

• When a recipe states to roll out the sugar, flower or modelling paste "quite thinly", roll out the kneaded paste until it is about 2–3mm/$\frac{1}{16}$–$\frac{1}{8}$in thick.

• When a recipe states to roll out the sugar, flower or modelling paste until it is 5mm/$\frac{1}{4}$in thick, you will find that marzipan spacers are extremely useful.

Designs, Guides and Templates

To use the templates, trace the outline of the template onto thin card, then carefully cut it out with a pair of scissors. To use the designs, simply trace each one onto a sheet of paper or thin card. To download printable versions visit www.dbp.co.uk/icingonthecake

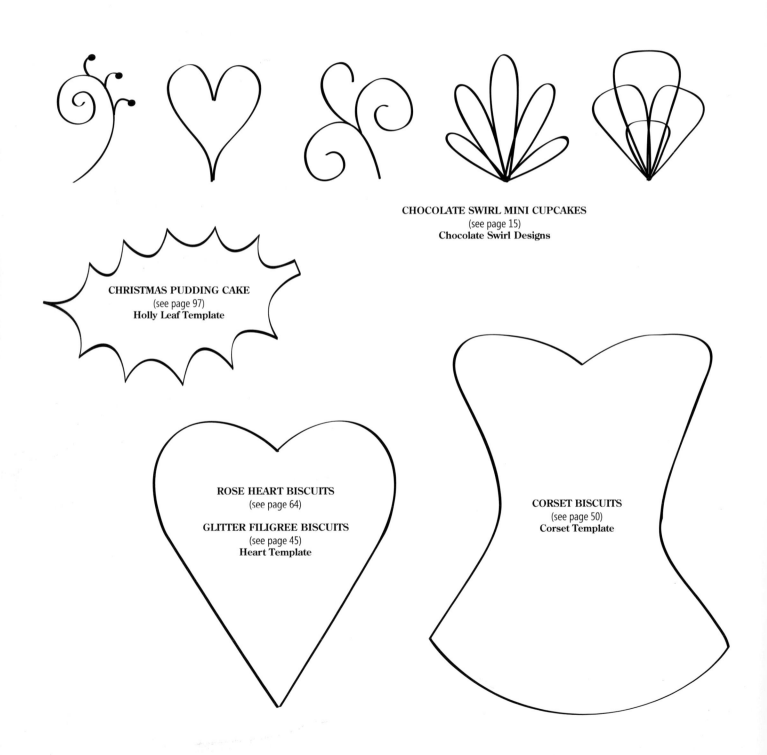

CHOCOLATE SWIRL MINI CUPCAKES
(see page 15)
Chocolate Swirl Designs

CHRISTMAS PUDDING CAKE
(see page 97)
Holly Leaf Template

ROSE HEART BISCUITS
(see page 64)

GLITTER FILIGREE BISCUITS
(see page 45)
Heart Template

CORSET BISCUITS
(see page 50)
Corset Template

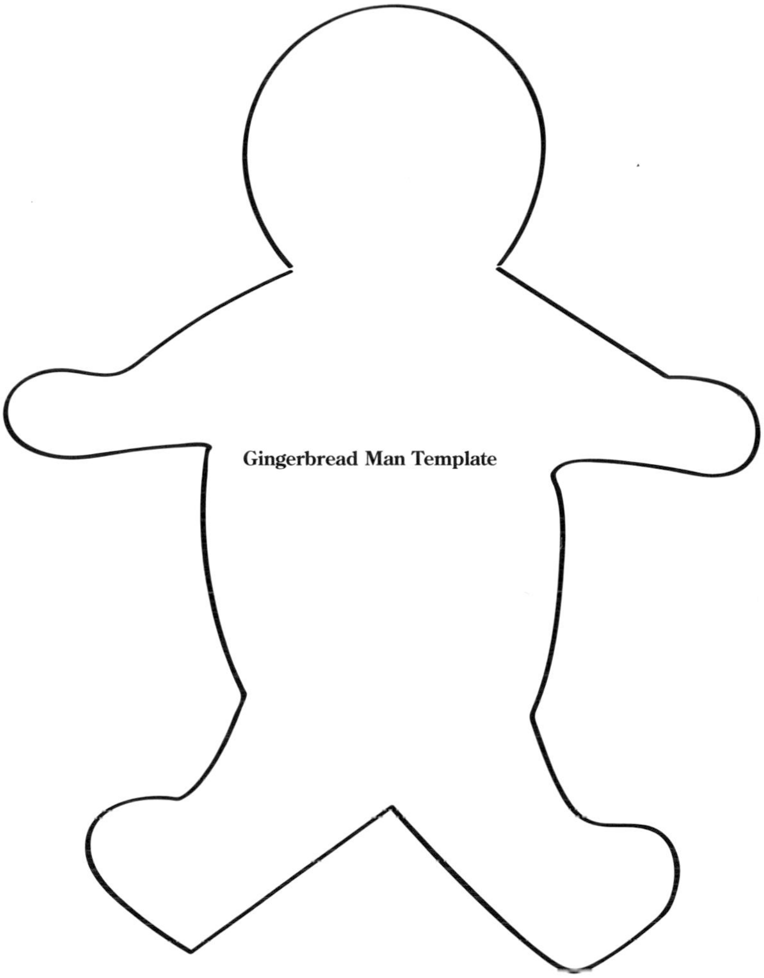

Gingerbread Man Template

Gingerbread Girl Template

GINGERBREAD FAMILY
page 25

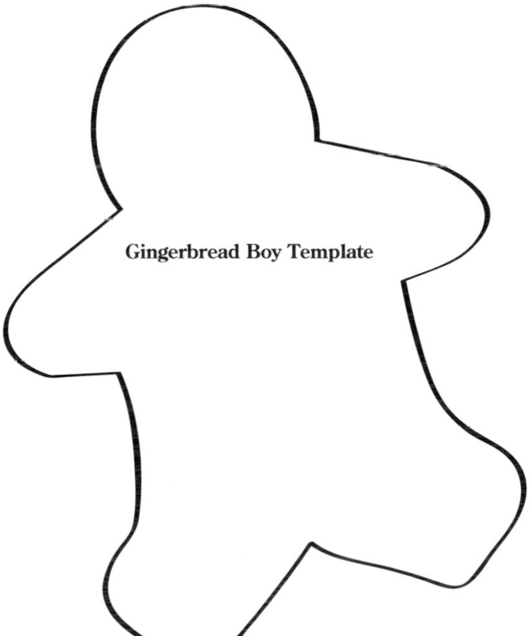

Gingerbread Boy Template

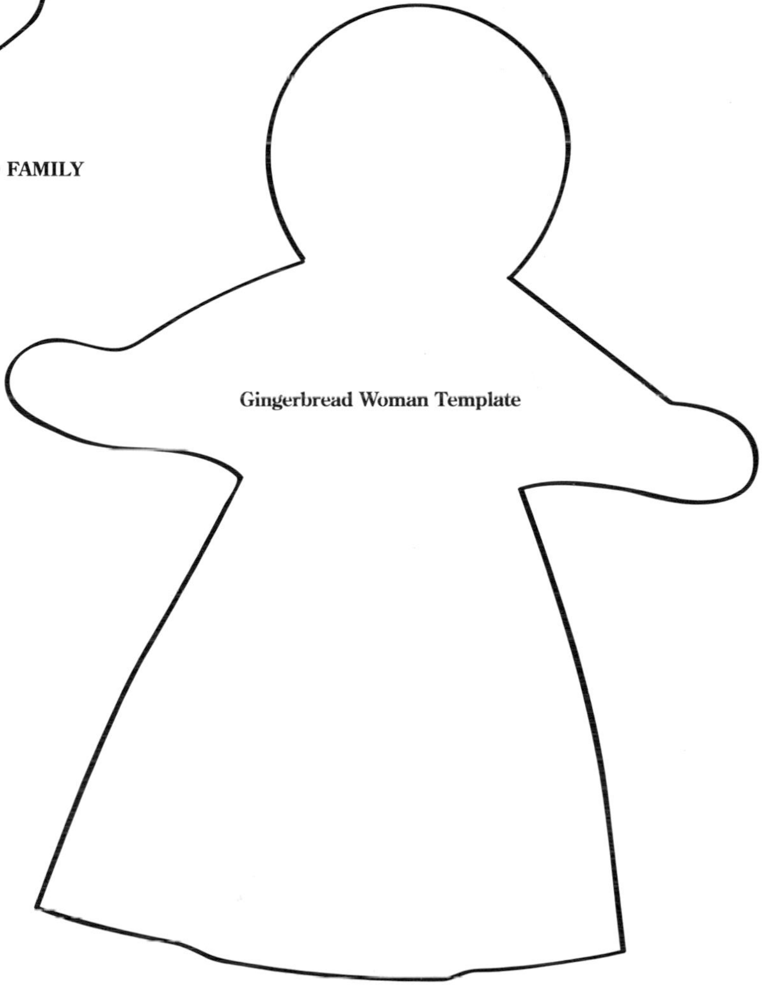

Gingerbread Woman Template

To use the templates, trace the outline of the template onto thin card, then carefully cut it out with a pair of scissors. To download printable versions visit www.dbp.co.uk/icingonthecake

DRAGON CAKE
(see page 74)

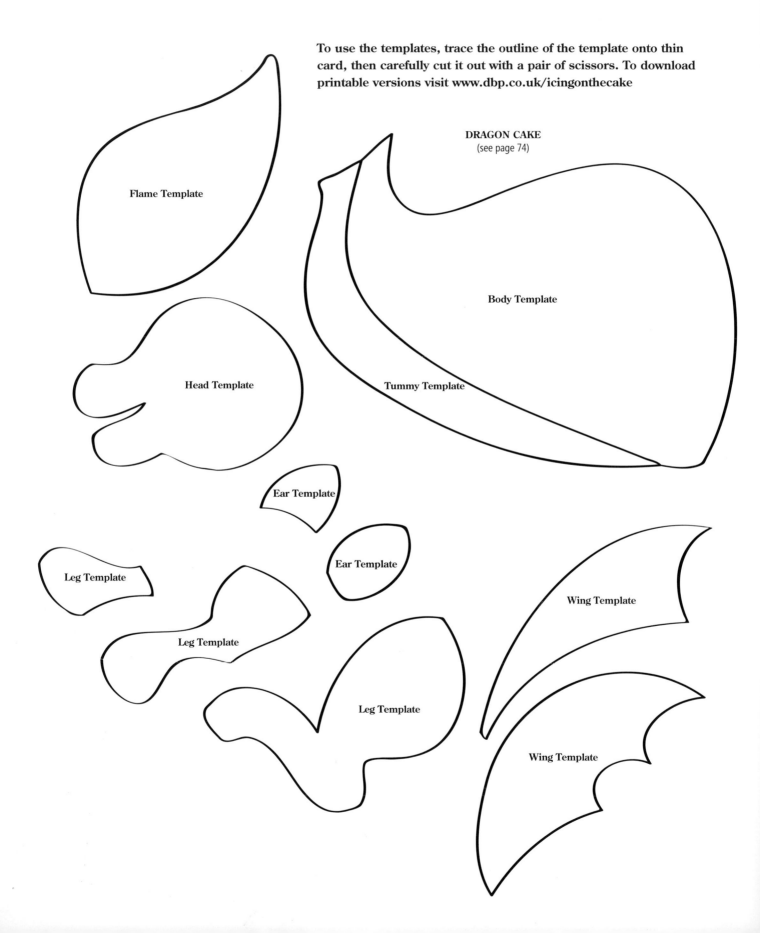

Flame Template

Body Template

Head Template

Tummy Template

Ear Template

Ear Template

Leg Template

Leg Template

Leg Template

Wing Template

Wing Template

WEDDING FAVOUR BLOSSOM BISCUITS
(see page 58)
Blossom Templates

Loop Piece Template

Tailpiece Template

Bow Join Template

ORANGE POMANDER CAKE
(see page 94)

GIFT-WRAPPED CAKE
(see page 135)

IVORY CORSAGE WEDDING CAKE
(see page 114)
Corsage and Leaf Templates

CHRISTMAS WREATH TREE
DECORATIONS
(see page 72)
Wreath Template

To use the templates, trace the outline of the template onto thin card, then carefully cut it out with a pair of scissors. To use the designs, simply trace each one onto a sheet of paper or thin card. To download printable versions visit www.dbp.co.uk/icingonthecake

Roof Panel Template

Side Wall Template

GINGERBREAD HOUSE
(see page 78)

Heart Template

End Wall Template

Door Template

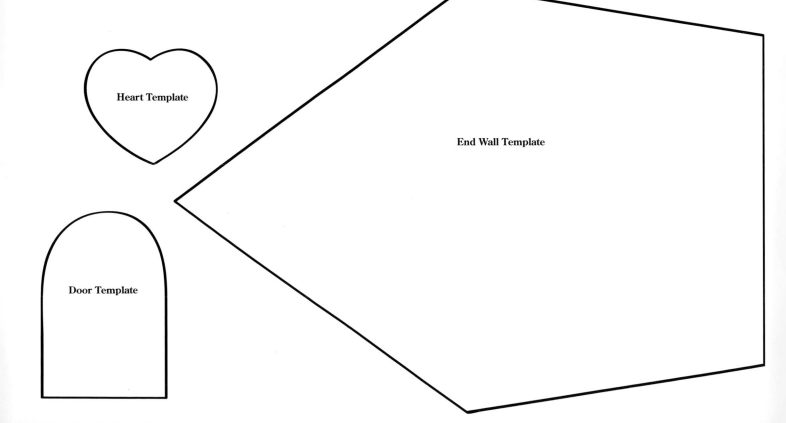

Circle Template

**THANKSGIVING
BISCUITS**
(see page 83)

**Thanksgiving Leaf
Designs**

**CHOCOLATE BOX CAKE
WITH TRUFFLES**
(see page 52)
**Flower, Leaf and Gift Tag
Templates**

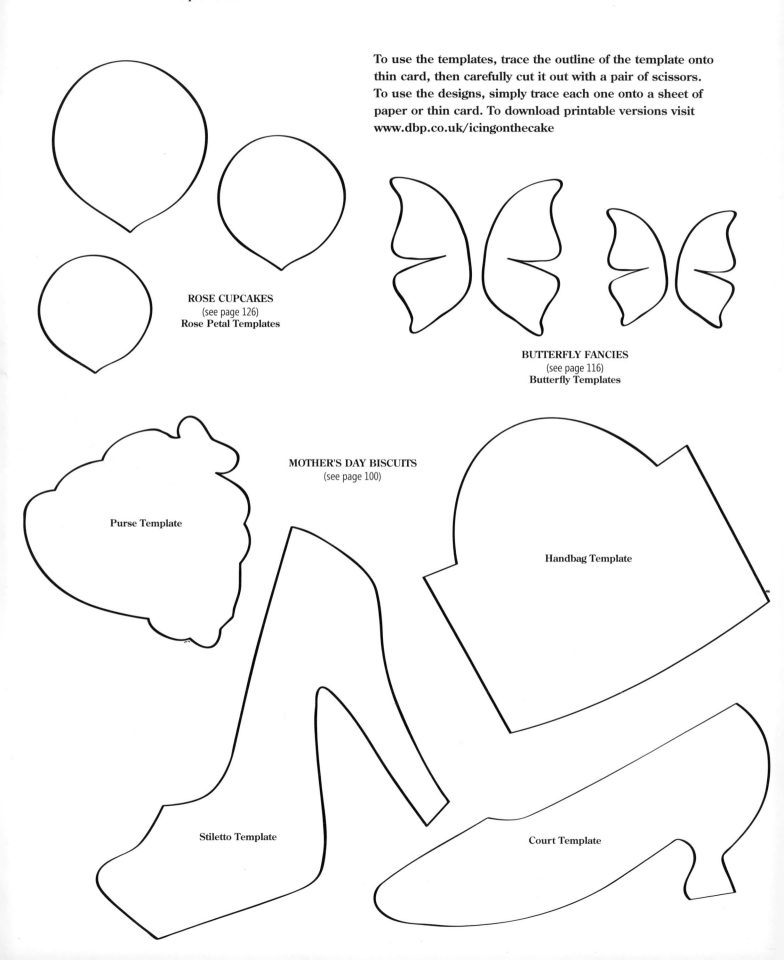

To use the templates, trace the outline of the template onto thin card, then carefully cut it out with a pair of scissors. To use the designs, simply trace each one onto a sheet of paper or thin card. To download printable versions visit www.dbp.co.uk/icingonthecake

ROSE CUPCAKES
(see page 126)
Rose Petal Templates

BUTTERFLY FANCIES
(see page 116)
Butterfly Templates

MOTHER'S DAY BISCUITS
(see page 100)

Purse Template

Handbag Template

Stiletto Template

Court Template

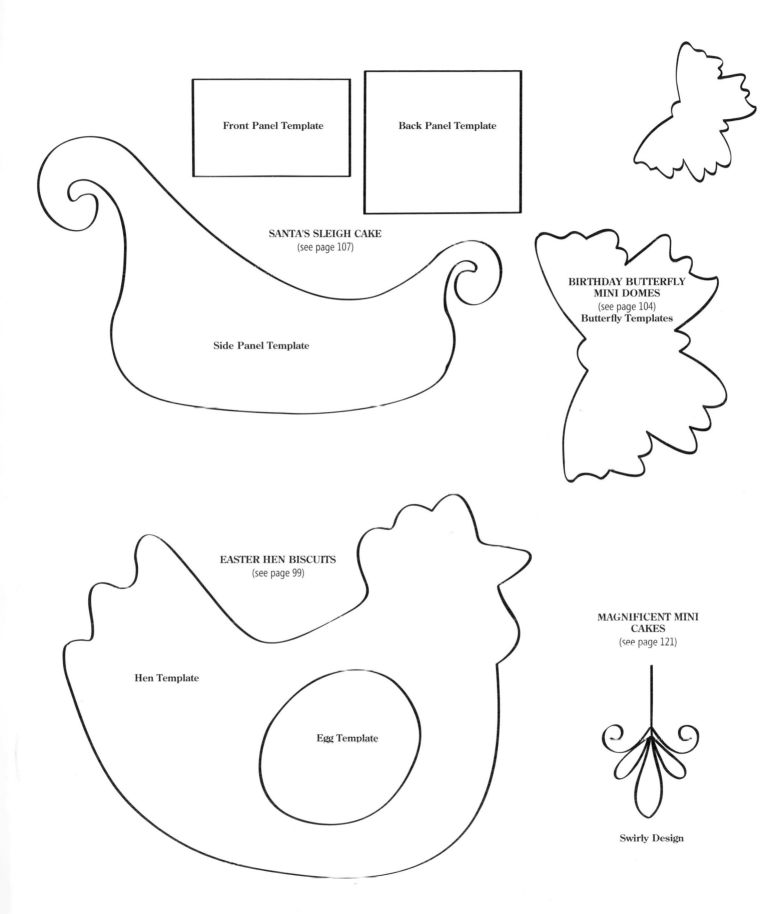

Front Panel Template

Back Panel Template

SANTA'S SLEIGH CAKE
(see page 107)

Side Panel Template

**BIRTHDAY BUTTERFLY
MINI DOMES**
(see page 104)
Butterfly Templates

EASTER HEN BISCUITS
(see page 99)

Hen Template

Egg Template

**MAGNIFICENT MINI
CAKES**
(see page 121)

Swirly Design

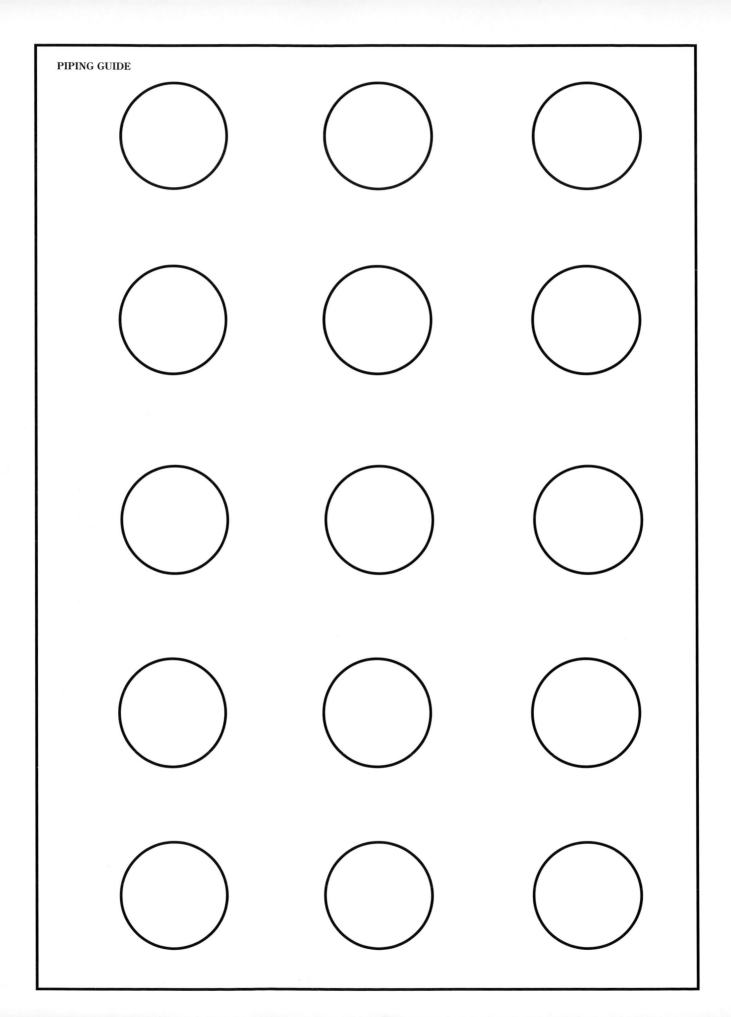

PIPING GUIDE

To use these guides, simply trace each one onto a sheet
of paper or thin card. To download printable versions visit
www.dbp.co.uk/icingonthecake

DOWELLING GUIDE

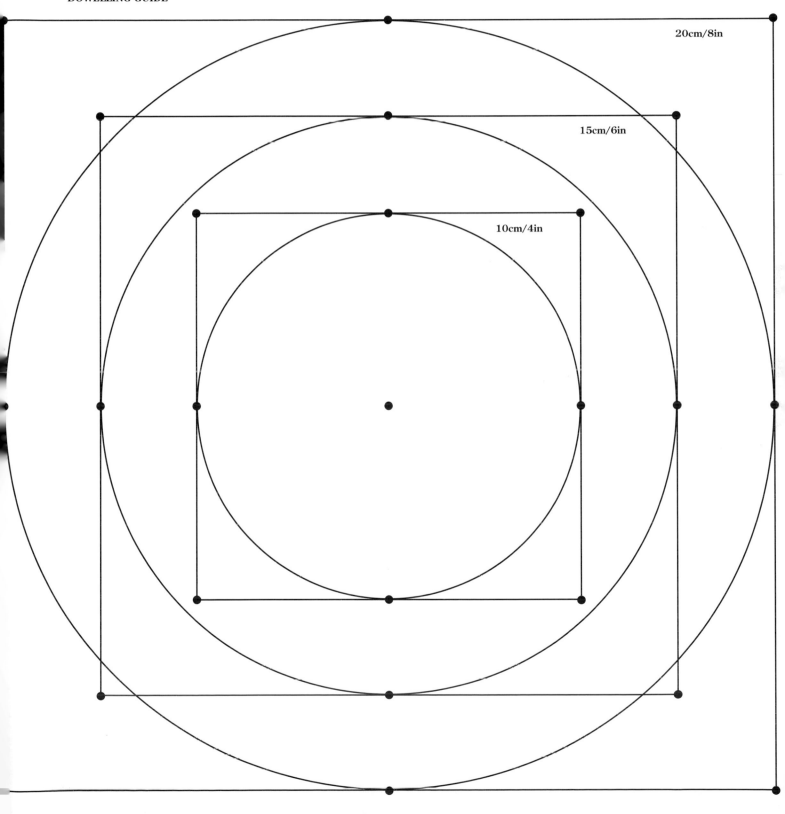

20cm/8in

15cm/6in

10cm/4in

Suppliers

BAKESTORE
Bakestore.co.uk
Tapsells Limited
Tapsells Lane
Wadhurst
East Sussex
TN5 6PL
Tel: +44 (0)1892 785735

CAKE CRAFT WORLD
www.cakecraftworld.co.uk
Unit 8, North Downs Business Park
Pilgrims Way (Lime Pit Lane)
Sevenoaks
Kent
TN13 2TL
Tel: +44 (0)1732 46 35 73

**CAKES, COOKIES &
CRAFTS SHOP**
www.cakescookiesandcraftshop.co.uk
Unit 2 Francis Business Park
White Lund Industrial Estate
Morecambe
Lancashire
LA3 3PT
Tel: +44 (0)1524 389684

**CAKE DECORATING
ACCESSORIES**
www.cakedecoratingaccessories.co.uk

CAKE STUFF
www.cake-stuff.com
Units 1-5, Gateside Ind. Estate
Lesmahagow, Lanarkshire
Scotland
ML11 0JR
Tel: +44 (0)1555 890111

JOHN LEWIS
www.johnlewis.com
Tel: +44 (0)8456 049 049

KIT BOX
www.kitbox.co.uk
Unit 3, Neads Court
Knowles Road
Clevedon
North Somerset
BS21 7XS
Tel: +44 (0)1275 879 030

LAKELAND
www.lakeland.co.uk
Tel: +44 (0)15394 88100

SQUIRES KITCHEN
www.squires-shop.com
Squires Group Squires House
3 Waverley Lane
Farnham
Surrey
GU9 8BB
Tel: +44 (0)845 61 71 810 or
   +44 (0)1252 260 260

SUGARSHACK
www.sugarshack.co.uk
Unit 12
Bowmans Trading Estate
Westmoreland Road
London NW9 9RL
Tel: +44 (0)20 8204 2994

WINDSOR CAKE CRAFT
www.windsorcakecraft.co.uk
211 Europa Boulevard
Gemini Business Park
Warrington
WA5 7TN
Tel: +44 (0)1925 444590

Index

Acknowledgments

What an adventure my first book has been and I have loved every minute of it. A mixture of fun and creativity – with a lot of hard work added in! I hope it will inspire you to try things that perhaps you thought you'd never be able to do.

My thanks to Grace Cheetham at Duncan Baird Publishers for giving me the opportunity to publish this book and for her encouragement and support; to Manisha Patel for her design talents and endless patience; to Krissy Mallett for her wonderful editing skills and bubbling enthusiasm (not to mention her fair hands as my "stunt double"); and to Alison Bolus and Georgine Waller who made sense of my initial text over hundreds of emails. Thank you also to my photographer, Jon Whitaker, for making it a very happy shoot and for his beautiful photographs; to Jon's assistants Thea, Ben and Simon; and to Lucy Harvey for her stylish props – many of which I wanted to take home to use myself!

Over the last year I have, on occasions, been somewhat elusive in the family home, and so a huge thanks goes to my husband, Colin, and our sons, Sam and Ben, for their love and understanding while I wrote this book. Thanks too to the rest of my family – my Mum, Valerie, and Dad, John Miller, my sister, Leigh Miller, brother, James Miller and his wife, Michelle, for all their help and input. Thanks also to friends in the village, Laura Carter and Sarah Jones, who were there at the beginning, and to Martha Allfrey, for her encouragement and inspiration (particularly when it came to the brownie recipe). And thanks to all those who have helped along the way: Polly Hawkins, Jemma Morgan, Annie Meston, Emily Van Eesteren and Sara Broome to name but a few.

Thank you all… x